Out Franklin Road

Out Franklin Road
The Oak Hill Home of Nashville's First Presbyterian Church

William C. Caruso

First Presbyterian Church of Nashville
Nashville, Tennessee

Dedication

This book is dedicated to Ophelia Thompson Paine, whose own history book, *Glen Leven Farm: A Family Story*, was inspirational in the decision to write this book. She has been a constant encourager and friend along the way. Moreover, two strong women ancestors of Ophelia played important roles in the history I have written. Kate Thompson Kirkman and Mary McConnell Overton Thompson, between them, once owned every square inch of the current property of First Presbyterian Church of Nashville. I am grateful for all three of these strong Thompson women.

Out Franklin Road: The Oak Hill Home of Nashville's First Presbyterian Church.
Copyright © 2023 First Presbyterian Church of Nashville. All rights reserved.

Out Franklin Road: The Oak Hill home of Nashville's First Presbyterian Church/ William C. Caruso. First printing.

ISBN-13: 979-8-218-17258-9

Book production (copy-editing, interior layout and design, and book cover) by
Tree of Life Memoirs
Hardeeville, South Carolina 29927
www.TreeofLifeMemoirs.com

Image of church steeple located on title page and book cover courtesy of First Presbyterian Church of Nashville Church Archives.

Printed by IngramSpark.

Published by First Presbyterian Church of Nashville
4815 Franklin Pike
Nashville, Tennessee 37220

Contents

	Dedication	v
	Preface	ix
1.	**Before 1796 and Tennessee Statehood**	**1**
	The French and Indian War	1
	The Move Westward	3
	The Maxwell Land Grants	8
	Who Were the Heirs of David Maxwell?	10
2.	**The Overton Years: 1796 Onward**	**13**
	Judge John Overton	14
	Purchase of Land Grant #367 and Development of Travellers Rest	16
	Important Historical Occurrences at Travellers Rest	18
	Overton and the Creation of Memphis	20
	John Overton Jr.	21
	Travellers Rest During the Civil War	22
	Overton Property Parceled Out	26
3.	**Van Leer Kirkman's Purchase & Era: 1887–1923**	**29**
	Van Leer Kirkman	31
	First Marriage and Family Controversy	32
	Second Marriage—to a Socialite	33
	The Move to Franklin Pike	37
	The Hermitage Stud Enterprise and Other Business Deals	39
	Oak Hill and the Centennial Exposition	43
	Kate Kirkman's Leadership and the Floral Parade	44
	The Sale of Oak Hill	49
4.	**Rogers Caldwell's Time: 1925–1929**	**51**
	Family Background	53
	Rogers Caldwell's Rise to Wealth and Power	55
	The Crash of 1929 and the Fall of Caldwell's Empire	57
5.	**The Cheek Family: 1929–1949**	**59**
	Frank L. Cheek	59

    Connecting the Dots   61
    The Sale of Oak Hill Farm to John Hancock Cheek   61

6. First Presbyterian Church of Nashville: 1949 to Present   **71**
    The Journey Toward Buying the Property   71
        Tensions in the 1940s—Catalysts for Change   72
        A Need for Change and the Building Survey Committee   75
        The Decision to Renovate and Expand Services   77
    Using the New Property   79
    Relocating the Congregation   80
        A Church Divided   81
        Moving Pains and Decisions   83
        Major Buildings and Projects: 1934–2022   88

7. Take a Look Around   **95**
    The First Presbyterian Church Flagpole   95
    Franklin Road/Franklin Pike   96
    John Overton High School   98
    Judson Baptist Church   98
    Holy Trinity Greek Orthodox Church   98
    Tyne Boulevard   100
    The Treemont Development on Tyne   100
    Kirkman Lane/the Bridle Path   101
    850 Tyne Boulevard   103
    Oak Hill Valley Subdivision   103
    Robertson Academy School   105
    The Sumner Property   110
    Franklin Road Academy   113

Appendices
Appendix A: How the Glen Leven Farm Thompsons and
Oak Hill Farm Kirkmans Were Related   115
Appendix B: The Pastors of 4815 Franklin Road   117
Appendix C: Text of North Carolina Land Grant #367   121

Notes   **123**
Bibliography   133
Index   137

About the Author   145

Preface

Out Franklin Road: The Oak Hill Home of Nashville's First Presbyterian Church is a brief historical study of a tract of land, varying from sixty-plus acres to 368 acres or so, in southern Davidson County, Tennessee. Because Davidson County and Nashville have been one entity—the Metropolitan Government of Nashville and Davidson County—since a 1962 vote, these acres are about Nashville, too, and they always have been. This land was first designated and owned by individuals who came into the area to create and grow the "Cumberland settlements" of Middle Tennessee. Nashville was one of these 1780s settlements. Currently, First Presbyterian Church of Nashville owns about 60 acres of the original tract. Even in the 1700s, Presbyterians were walking on these acres. Part of the remarkable history of this land is the recurrent ownership by people who were part of First Presbyterian Church well before the church purchased the property in 1949. It is hoped that this history of the property, and the neighboring properties, will be a useful companion to the church's other written narratives.

Many brief histories of First Presbyterian Church have been written; all can be found in the church's archives. Two comprehensive histories have been written in the modern day, telling the story in great detail. One is *The First Presbyterian Church of Nashville: A Documentary History* by Wilbur F. Creighton Jr. and Leland Johnson, eds. (1986). The other is *First Church: A History of Nashville First Presbyterian Church*, volumes 1, 2, and 3 by Damaris Witherspoon Steele (2004, 2005). This current book seeks not to tell the church's history again, though an obvious overlap occurs in the story of First Presbyterian buying the suburban property in 1949, then moving the entire operation of the church in 1955. The book will also show the influence of two large estates, both named Oak Hill. Indeed, the whole section of the county in and around those estates came to be known as the Oak Hill neighborhood.

Moreover, the name was chosen in 1952 when the neighborhood incorporated itself into the small City of Oak Hill in Davidson County. When the metropolitan city/county government was launched in 1962, Oak Hill continued as a satellite city within the overall metro structure. The sweep of history from North Carolina Land Grant #367 to today's 4815 Franklin Road is full of interesting people and significant events. I hope that this little history will be useful and fun for both the casual reader and the historian.

Many people were helpful in the writing of this book. I acknowledge as many as possible and apologize to those I may have forgotten. I could not have produced this book without the capable staff members at the Tennessee State Library and Archives and the Metro Archives of Nashville and Davidson County. Allison Griffey and Trent Hanner at TSLA were always gracious and helpful. Among these professionals, Kelley Sirko of Metro Archives is the shining star of this book. During the unfortunate Covid-19 pandemic, which greatly slowed the research part of the book, Kelley provided ways to communicate with me and to send information and digital images for those many months when things were locked down. No praise is high enough for her contribution. At Travellers Rest, I benefitted from personal meetings with Jennifer Butt and Lauren Batte. Ridley Wills II was graciously helpful through his wonderful Nashville Pikes history books and in personal contacts.

A remarkable number of living people are actually related to some of the characters in my story; those serendipities certainly made the research more fun. I am grateful to Kip Gayden, Will and Cissy Caldwell Akers, Meredith Caldwell III ("Duc"), Andrew Byrd, Jim Kay of the Battle of Nashville Trust, Allen and Frances Bryan, James Baker, Duncan McKay Fort, Nancy (Mrs. William H. Jr.) Eason, Hill McAlister, John and Mary Earthman, Lavinia Jones Fillebrown, Dr. Clinton J. Holloway, Kim Sumner Hardin, Patricia Potter McDonald, Fletch Coke, and the late Charlie Cardwell, who provided my introduction to the world of the Davidson County Register of Deeds office. I would have been lost in the wilderness without the guidance of Patricia West through this whole publication process. Her expertise in layout, cover design, formatting of text, and grammar have made the book be more than "words on a page." Similarly, the folks at IngramSpark were so very helpful.

Helpful in quite another way was my spouse, Bekah, who ended up giving up the dining room table for several years while research and writing went on. Without her patience and support, the book would not have happened, and I owe her a great debt of gratitude.

Chapter One

Before 1796 and Tennessee Statehood

The French and Indian War

A story must start somewhere. This story will begin in 1754, some twenty-five years before Nashville's 1779 founding, with an explanation of how "the Cumberland settlements"—the frontier outposts along the Cumberland River that one day would be Nashville—came into being.[1] At that time, North America was a wilderness, hardly settled very far inland from the Atlantic seaboard. European powers, chiefly Great Britain, France, and Spain, were mounting exploratory expeditions to map out and claim inland New World territories. France was a power in what became Canada and was intent on moving southward. Great Britain controlled most of the Atlantic coast and sought westward expansion. Spain's influence was in the Gulf Coast and New Orleans areas. Caught in between these ambitious powers were numerous Native American Indian tribes. By conquest, cooperation, and a combination of these, the Europeans made inroads and claimed outposts; yet territorial disputes were the rule, not the exception.

By 1754, open hostilities between Great Britain and France had already erupted in North America. The Ohio Company, a development enterprise in Virginia, was claiming large areas of future Virginia, West Virginia, Pennsylvania, Indiana, and more for Great Britain. At the same time, France, from its Montreal base, was claiming much of the same territory. In a move to assert Virginia's claims, Robert Dinwiddie, Royal Governor of the Virginia colony, commissioned twenty-one-year-old

George Washington as a Major in the militia and sent him forth to demand that the French leave the area. Dinwiddie was a major investor in the Ohio Company; thus, his reasons to oust the French were both official and personal. Unfortunately, the confrontation did not go well. At a 1753 meeting with a French official near Erie, Pennsylvania, young Washington was politely rebuffed and sent away.

The following year, armed with a better plan and 150 soldiers, Major Washington was dispatched to the very important mouth of the Ohio River, where the Allegheny and Monongahela Rivers came together—today's Pittsburgh. The French had built Fort Duquesne there. The importance of this particular area was incalculable because the Ohio River flowed to the Mississippi River, and whoever controlled these waters controlled all of North America from an economic standpoint. After a brief skirmish, Washington was forced to retreat south, where he hastily built a small outpost given the name Fort Necessity. There he prepared for another battle with the French. It soon came, Washington's forces were humiliated, and the little Fort Necessity was burned. Embarrassed and discouraged, Washington returned home and resigned his commission. The world had not seen the last of Washington, though. In 1755, he returned to the Ohio frontier as a volunteer, serving with distinction under General George Braddock. As a result of his bravery and leadership, he was commissioned again and given the rank of Lt. Colonel. In addition, he was given the whole Virginia Regiment to command.

The 1754 engagements triggered what became known in North America as the French and Indian War; in Europe, these events became part of a multi-nation struggle known as the Seven Years' War. Great Britain and France dispatched great armies to North America. The numerous Native American Indian tribes allied with both sides, depending on their perception of what alliances would be best for their purposes. Many, or most, tribes allied with the French, the perception being that the French had in previous years been focused on fur trapping and trade, while the English had a reputation of seeking to appropriate land for settling.

This conflict ended in 1763 with the Treaty of Paris, only one of several world treaties in history that have borne that title. As the struggle concluded, France was defeated by the British and effectively disappeared from North America, giving up Canada and all its interests in the Great Lakes and the Ohio Valley areas. French holdings West of the Mississippi River went to Spain (in later years, this Louisiana Territory would come back to the French, eventually to be bought by the United States as the Louisiana Purchase.) Spain gave up Florida to the British but got Cuba back.

So, by 1763, Great Britain controlled everything on the Atlantic Coast from Hudson Bay in New York to the Florida Keys. One could say that, for all its complexities, a major result of the French and Indian War was this: Great Britain now had a clear opportunity for westward expansion, a most valuable prize. The road forward, however, was not to be easy.

The Move Westward

The year 1763 proved to be significant in another way. To make good on promises and alliances made in the just-ended war, King George III and his Privy Council in England issued the Proclamation of 1763, which, among other things, forbade land dealings with Native American Indian tribes to the west of the thirteen British colonies. A North-South boundary line at the western borders of the colonies marked the line beyond which no attempts to buy Indian lands would be made. Essentially, the Appalachian Mountains marked this line. Land to the west was to be reserved for tribal hunting purposes.

Nevertheless, England was a long way off, and enforcement was never really possible. The defeated French had been desirous of hunting and trapping, but the English colonists were more interested in acquiring land for settling.[2] Eager land speculators sensed the mood of adventurers and families to pick up and move into the uncharted wilderness, rumored to be fertile for farming and full of game for hunting. In the case of what would become Tennessee, they began to come chiefly from Pennsylvania, Virginia, and, of course, North Carolina.[3]

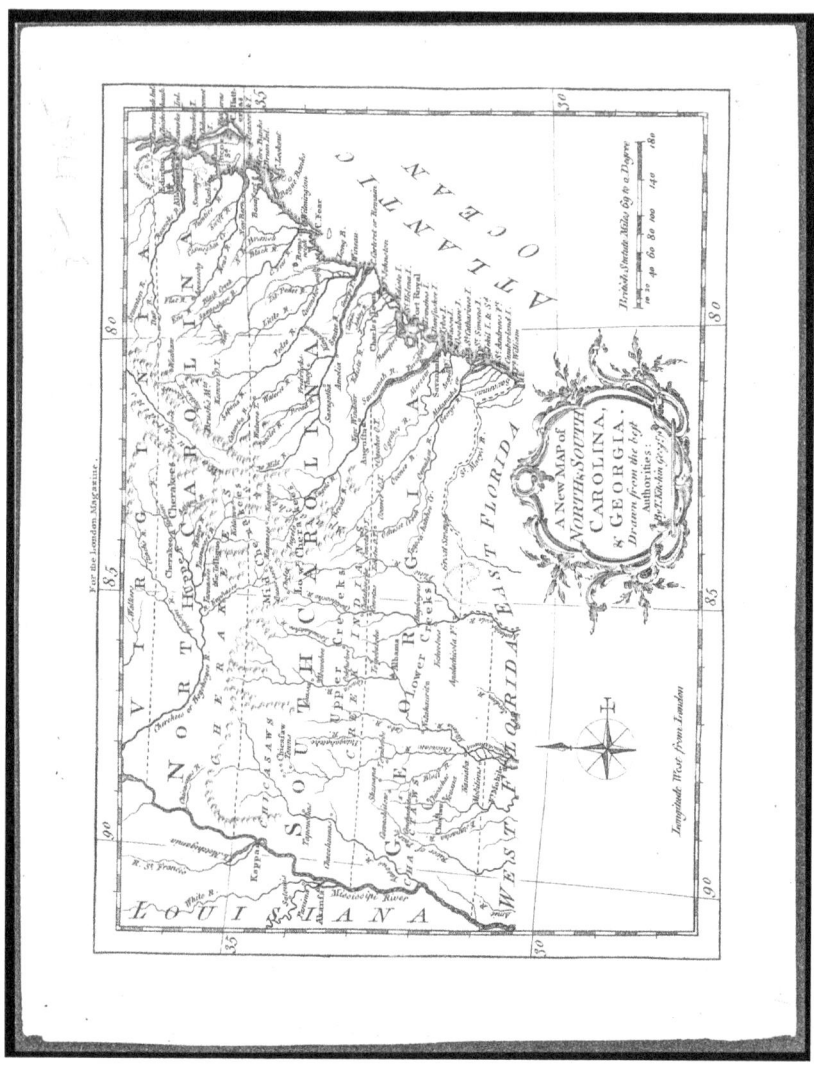

English map of the lower Atlantic colonies, 1765. This is how the English viewed their New World holdings, with Atlantic colonies stretching far westward. Courtesy of Tennessee State Library and Archives.

North Carolina Military District, established 1782. Land grants for revolutionary soldiers and early settlers were awarded in this western district of North Carolina. Courtesy of Tennessee State Library and Archives.

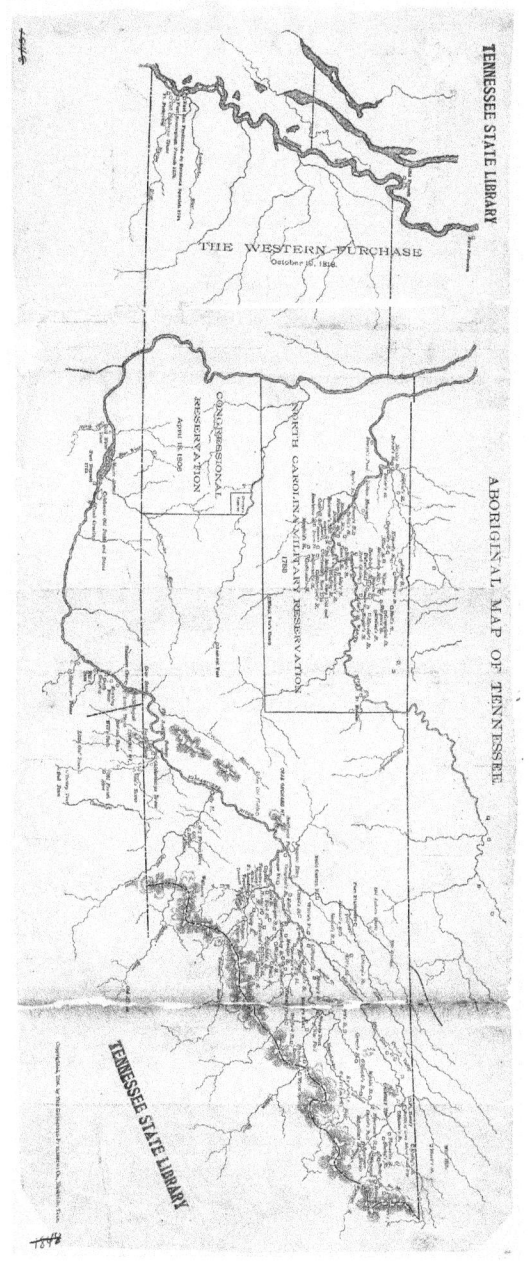

The landmark event in the move west was the establishment of settlements on the Watauga, Holston, and Nolichucky Rivers, near present-day Elizabethton, Tennessee. The first permanent settlers in this area, William Bean, followed by Daniel Boone, established themselves in 1769 at the Sycamore Shoals of the Watauga River.[4] James Robertson, who later would become known as the Father of Middle Tennessee, moved from Wake County, North Carolina, in 1770 to the new settlement. His family sought out this Western area of North Carolina, beyond the Appalachians, because of increasing aggravation with Great Britain's administration of its American colonies.

Several settlers from Virginia actually thought they were settling in Virginia due to the primitive state of boundary surveying in these uncharted areas of North Carolina. In the fall of 1771, Anthony Bledsoe surveyed a boundary line between Britain's Virginia and North Carolina colonies and determined that the Watauga settlements were in North Carolina. That meant they were illegally on Cherokee lands, and because of the Proclamation of 1763, British agents ordered the settlers to leave. However, James Robertson and John Sevier began to devise ways to lease, not buy, Indian land. One way involved the formation of the Watauga Association.

In 1772, the Watauga Association was formed through an official document of agreement between settlers. "The political history of what was to become Tennessee began with this meeting."[5] Unfortunately, its articles of incorporation no longer exist, but the 1780 Cumberland Compact of the Cumberland Settlement is said to be very similar, creating a colony for mutual benefit and protection. In 1774, the settlers leased the land they had already settled from the Cherokees.

The Wataugans were often referred to as the Overmountain Colony; that is, the colony on the western side of the Appalachians. A few years later, these Overmountain Men, as they were dubbed, would make a name for themselves at the 1780 Battle of Kings Mountain.

In 1775, the very significant Treaty of Sycamore Shoals was accomplished. Sycamore Shoals refers to a rocky stretch of the Watauga River in today's Elizabethton, Tennessee. This area was said to have strategic military value to both Cherokees and settlers. Here, Richard

Henderson met with Cherokees and negotiated the purchase of millions of acres of Cherokee land, described as "much of Kentucky and a good chunk of Tennessee."[6] More clearly, it was all the land between the Kentucky and the Cumberland Rivers. The purchase included the land already settled by the Watauga group and the territory that would become the Cumberland settlements in Middle Tennessee.

Representing the Cherokee tribe was the old Chief Attakullakulla. Henderson and Daniel Boone represented the white settlers. Dragging Canoe, the old chief's son, was vehemently opposed to the transaction his father was about to make, arguing that the Cherokees were bartering away their heritage and their future. He famously predicted a "dark and bloody" future for all concerned.[7] Dragging Canoe eventually broke with his father, traveling south with other dissident Cherokees. They formed towns along the route to what is now Chattanooga, as well as a new tribe, the Chickamauga. Along with other Cherokees, they became fierce opponents of the settlers who came to the Cumberland in Middle Tennessee.

By all accounts, neither Attakullakulla nor Richard Henderson was authorized to strike the Treaty of Sycamore Shoals. Henderson had in mind to create a new American colony, Transylvania, from the millions of acres he obtained. However, neither Virginia nor North Carolina approved the treaty and annulled it. Still, Henderson himself was given over 200,000 acres of land by the colonies involved.

Undaunted, Henderson continued plans for the Western expansion of white settlements. He began to organize groups to go all the way to the Cumberland River, following up on reports of early fur traders, among them Timothy Demonbreun, that the Cumberland area would be a good place to establish settlements. In 1779, while the War for Independence was still being fought, Henderson and his Transylvania Company put together settler expeditions to push westward.

James Robertson was tapped to lead a group of men overland to the Cumberland, while John Donelson was authorized to conduct a flotilla of small boats to the same area. Robertson had earlier taken a group of men over there, leaving three men behind to guard the encampment while he returned to the Watauga to prepare for a larger expedition.

Donelson's group included the families of Robertson's men and other families. Both groups left from Fort Patrick Henry, along the Holston River, in what is now Kingsport, Tennessee.

Among those in the Donelson flotilla of about 30 to 40 boats were Jesse Maxwell and family. We do not know the makeup of that family; we sorely wish we did. Knowing their names would answer many questions relevant to this research. The names of those in the Donelson party are inscribed on a bronze plaque now displayed in the lobby of the Metropolitan Nashville Courthouse. The Watauga Cumberland Settlers Association commissioned the plaque and dedicated it on April 24, 1910, precisely one hundred and thirty years from the day Donelson's boats arrived in Nashville. A big ceremony in downtown Nashville was held on April 24, 1880, the centennial.[8] The plaque was not dedicated until 1910 (the Settlers' Association was not founded until 1906).[9]

Jesse Maxwell's name on the plaque placed him definitively in the Cumberland Settlements in 1780. This Jesse Maxwell is directly responsible for securing the land which would one day become the Franklin Road property of the First Presbyterian Church of Nashville. Yet even his name on a plaque does not nearly answer all the questions that arise about Jesse Maxwell and his family.

The Maxwell Land Grants

On January 16, 1783, this Jesse Maxwell was granted a preemption of 640 acres of land by the province of North Carolina for himself and another 640-acre tract for the "Heirs of David Maxwell."[10] As far as we can tell, David was the brother of Jesse Maxwell. Preemptions and land grants open a new chapter in the history of North Carolina and Tennessee in general, and Middle Tennessee in particular. These grants came about as a solution to the knotty problem of North Carolina being practically broke in the waning years of the Revolutionary War. The province was "short of funds but in dire need of a military force."[11] What that government had plenty of was land because, in theory, North Carolina's territory stretched from its Atlantic coastline westward to the Mississippi River and beyond. West of the Appalachian

Mountains lay millions of acres of unexplored and uncleared land. So the provincial government created a system that awarded land in lieu of cash payments, 640 acres at a time. A 640-acre tract was easily measured, for it represents a square one mile on each side. This was a commonly used method of measuring land holdings. Such a tract was also called (and still is) a section. Thirty-six sections made up a township. Soldiers needed to have served at least two years to qualify for the grant; furthermore, the higher the rank, the more land in the grant. An army private was awarded the basic 640 acres. Part of the preemption in the name of the heirs of David Maxwell would, in 155 years, become the First Presbyterian Church of Nashville property.

The place chosen for these land awards was in the Cumberland area of North Carolina's western district, the land bounding the Cumberland River. Settling of the area had already begun there with the 1779–80 arrival of the James Robertson and John Donelson groups. In 1782, the North Carolina Legislature set the boundaries for a military reservation, also called the military district. The exact boundary began

> … where the Cumberland River crosses the Virginia line [now the Kentucky/Virginia line] running South 55 miles, then West to the Tennessee River, down the river and back to the Virginia [now Kentucky] state line, and East along that line to the beginning.[12]

Before the reservation could be set aside for soldiers, there was the situation of settlers already within the reservation. So, the North Carolina Legislature decided to appoint three commissioners—Anthony Bledsoe, Isaac Shelby, and Absolom Tatum—to survey the reservation's boundaries and to settle with and grant preemption certificates to those who were already settled within the boundaries. Each head of a family and each male over twenty-one years of age living on the land before June 1, 1780, was entitled to a grant of 640 acres.[13] According to the Maxwell family history, Jesse Maxwell, in 1780–81, accompanied the military district surveyors.[14]

North Carolina archive records show us that Commissioners Tatum and Bledsoe, by their Transaction #159 on January 16, 1783, documented that:

> Jesse Maxwell obtained a preemption of 640 acres of land lying on the West Side of Mill Creek about 2.5 miles from Roger Topp's land and along a buffalo road leading toward the South and including a spring marked DM, which runs into the West fork of Mill Creek to begin a quarter of a mile westward from the spring and to the Northeast for quantity.

On the same day, Jesse Maxwell obtained, in Transaction #161, for the Heirs of David Maxwell, a preemption of 640 acres of land lying on the West fork of Mill Creek, joining the western boundary of Jesse Maxwell's land, including two small springs.[15] It is impossible to say with certainty whether Jesse Maxwell was granted a preemption because he was a resident in the Cumberland settlement before June 1, 1780, or because he fought in the army. He is clearly listed among the patriots who fought the British at the Battle of Kings Mountain, South Carolina, on October 7, 1780. Official records show Jesse Maxwell as a Private in both the Infantry and the Cavalry of North Carolina.[16]

Who Were the Heirs of David Maxwell?

We wish we could know more about David Maxwell. Was he with the Jesse Maxwell family on the Donelson voyage in 1780? We don't know for sure. We do know that he signed the Cumberland Compact in 1780, but Jesse did not. Is that because David chose to stay in the Cumberland settlement, but Jesse did not? According to records, Jesse Maxwell did not marry until about 1787, so his wife and children were not with him on the Donelson voyage in 1780. Who, then, constituted Jesse's family? Did Jesse bring his parents—David Maxwell and Nellie McCullough Maxwell—from Lancaster, Pennsylvania, to the Cumberland settlement? No official record tells us such; however, the Claiborne memoir claims that Jesse Maxwell left Lancaster with his parents before 1750 and came to Virginia.[17]

David and Nellie Maxwell were said to be from County Donegal, Ireland; however, family records also state that they were from Scotland. Since County Donegal was one of the Irish counties which were a part of the Ulster Plantation experiment, this is entirely possible. In that experiment, Lowland Scots were brought to several counties in Ireland. These counties made up the Ulster Plantation. It was these Scots, living in Ireland for a time, who were known in America as the Scotch-Irish. These people came to America in great numbers when agriculture failed in Ireland.

David Maxwell, Jesse's brother, was killed by Indians in March 1781, in the Cumberland settlements, specifically near Mansker's Station (now Goodlettsville, Tennessee). All official historical records from North Carolina and Tennessee attest to this. The location of David's death seems to contradict the family tradition cited by Mollie Maxwell Claiborne, which says that Indians killed David on the Caney Fork River. Given that the Caney Fork is not close to Nashville by most standards, these contradictory records seem impossible to reconcile. However, there is a journal record of life in the Nashville settlement that describes one canoe trip to the Caney Fork, made by twenty men in search of game for the starving community. Efforts to place David Maxwell on that trip have not yielded any results, but the possibility remains. It is also possible that the records say Mansker's Station because he lived there at that Cumberland station, not because he was killed at that spot. The North Carolina state records of May 10, 1784, contain a long list of those killed in the settlements. David Maxwell is specifically listed with those granted land preemptions for being "killed in the settlement and defense of the County of Davidson."[18] It is also possible that the family record is wrong. One document says a George Maxwell was killed on the Caney Fork.

It does not appear possible to know more about David Maxwell beyond these facts, e.g., spouse or children. The clear thing is that Jesse Maxwell, on January 16, 1783, was granted a preemption for himself and an adjacent 640 acres for the heirs of David Maxwell. North Carolina records specifically name David Maxwell as deserving this land because of his service to the fledgling settlement. These heirs are named explicitly on deeds as William and Moses Maxwell. We presume they are David's children because they are also called Jesse's nephews in certain documents. In a now unlocatable document that the author has seen at either Tennessee State Library and Archives or the Metro Nashville Archives, this David Maxwell is referred to as the prime ancestor of his line of Maxwells, meaning the first ancestor to settle in Tennessee. This document says that David Maxwell was "born before 1750, in Virginia," and died between 1783–85 in Davidson County, Tennessee. It states that the known children of David Maxwell were William, Moses, and David Andrew Maxwell. This lost document presents problems that are unsolvable without more reliable information.

The byzantine process of getting from preemption to grant to registration in North Carolina, then to registration in Davidson County—not to mention arranging for a more specific survey of the 640 acres—ultimately meant that an actual land grant did not happen until June 26, 1793, when North Carolina Land Grant #367 was issued to the heirs of David Maxwell. (A copy of Land Grant #367 with that date can be found in the First Presbyterian Church of Nashville Archives.)

According to the Maxwell family history, the two sons of David Maxwell sold their land to Judge John Overton without ever seeing their land. They were said to have gone to an area near Cincinnati.[19]

Chapter Two

The Overton Years: 1796 Onward

The official date of Land Grant #367 to William and Moses Maxwell was June 26, 1793, a full ten years after the January 16, 1783, issuance of Jesse Maxwell's preemption and the preemption Jesse obtained for his brother David's heirs. (As an aside, 1783 is also the date that North Carolina created Davidson County, North Carolina.)

Since practically nothing is known of William and Moses Maxwell, we can only speculate about the decade of 1783–1793. Did these boys not reach adulthood until then? Were there complications in getting from preemption to grant? We know for sure that the grant process was not easy, but we just don't know where the boys were and what they were doing during that time. The Mollie Claiborne history of the Maxwells indicates that they were not on their land.

As joint heirs, William and Moses each had one-half ownership of the 640 acres of land. In two transactions, separated by a few years, they sold all the 640 acres of Land Grant #367 to Judge John Overton. Overton was one of the seven lawyers licensed in 1790 to practice in the Nashville area. He arrived in 1789 from Virginia by way of Kentucky; he was also a surveyor. In Nashville, he roomed at the home of John Donelson's widow, sharing a room with another young lawyer, Andrew Jackson.[1] Mrs. Donelson would eventually become Jackson's mother-in-law.

Judge John Overton

John Overton, born April 9, 1766, came from Brooksville, Louisa County, Virginia.[2] An ambitious young man, John left Virginia at the age of twenty for Danville, Kentucky; his older brother Waller had already gone there to develop land given to their father for service in the French and Indian War. In the manner of the time, he studied law with an older attorney and was active in the Danville Political Club, where, no doubt, he also learned about land speculation and profits to be made therein.[3]

> The most significant event of Overton's Danville residency was his acquaintance with Rachel Donelson Robards (later to become Mrs. Andrew Jackson.) Her stories of the Cumberland settlements, which her father helped to found, persuaded John to leave Kentucky for Nashville.[4]

The great portion of legal cases which came to those first seven lawyers in Nashville had to do with land disputes. Overton made these a specialty. This decision enabled him to keep abreast of government policies—current grants being issued to the choicest property locations, current values of land, and those tracts of land which could be cheaply purchased due to the owner's ignorance or financial difficulty.[5] John Overton made the most of the knowledge and experience he gained.

> For a man of frail physique and chronic illness, Overton was extremely enterprising. In addition to being one the finest land lawyers in the county, he was Supervisor of Federal Excise from 1795–96, Judge of the Tennessee Supreme Court from 1804–1810, Judge of the State Supreme Court of Errors and Appeals from 1811–1818, a banker, a land speculator, presidential campaign advisor for Andrew Jackson, a law teacher, a horticulturist, and a planter. He hosted civic affairs and social gatherings and controlled a newspaper, the *Nashville Gazette*.[6]

THE OVERTON YEARS 15

Judge John Overton. Courtesy of Travellers Rest Historic House Museum, Inc.

Judge John Overton's wife, Mary McConnell White May Overton. Her father, James White, was the founder of Knoxville, TN. She was a widow when she married Judge Overton. Courtesy of Travellers Rest Historic House Museum, Inc.

Purchase of Land Grant #367 and Development of Travellers Rest

Overton began to buy up land all over Tennessee. One of the areas he apparently had his eye on was just south of Nashville. On August 6, 1796, Overton purchased William Maxwell's half of the 640-acre Land Grant #367 for $1,066.66. In 1800, he bought Moses Maxwell's half for $1,480.00 (he had already paid Moses $200 during the William Maxwell transaction for "inequities.")[7] Thus, North Carolina Land Grant #367 became the central tract of land for what would become known as Travellers Rest. While digging foundations for a house, many buried Indian skeletons were found; artifacts with them helped modern archaeologists date the buried Indian village to between A.D. 1300 and 1500. These Indian bones moved Overton at first to name his plantation Golgotha, which, in Hebrew, is *place of the skulls*. It is not known precisely when he changed the name to Travellers Rest, but letters as early as 1815 used it as the return address.[8]

Evidence shows that Overton began farming operations on his land in 1797. House construction began in 1798 and finished in 1799 when he started to live there in the four-room dwelling. Official documents and signs always use the 1799 date as the beginning of the plantation's life. Scholars agree that the name Travellers Rest reflected Overton's hospitality. The name was not new to the area, however. James Robertson's home on Richland Creek had the same name.[9]

Overton quickly added acreage once he began to buy in the south-of-Nashville area. In fact, between the two Maxwell transactions, he purchased Land Grant #60, the Samuel Barton grant, a contiguous grant west of the Maxwell lands. And twice, Overton and Jesse Maxwell completed transactions of small pieces of land in the area between their grant lands. By 1830, Travellers Rest covered 2300 acres.[10] Moreover, by the end of Overton's first decade in Tennessee, he owned over 65,000 acres of land in Middle Tennessee.[11] Family lore has sometimes placed the acreage of Travellers Rest as between 3600 and 5000 acres, which cannot be accurate. Even so, John Overton's holdings across the state "made him probably the largest landowner in Tennessee, and one of the largest in the nation."[12]

Travellers Rest. The original 1799 house was only the right half of the house in the picture. The house today has been restored to reflect the period of John Overton's life. Later on, inheriting families added on to the exterior of the house, giving it a different appearance. Additions not known in Judge Overton's life have been removed. Courtesy of Travellers Rest Historic House Museum, Inc.

Travellers Rest was quite an agricultural operation. Cotton and tobacco were the chief money crops, but substantial amounts of corn, potatoes, peas, apples, grapes, and peaches were grown. The peach orchards were on a large hill about three-quarters of a mile northwest of the main house, between where today's Harding Place intersects Franklin Road and today's Interstate 65 interchange. Overton was a slaveholder, though not a large one by the standards of states where cotton was grown in more abundance. He owned eighteen slaves in 1816 and about fifty at his death in 1833.[13]

The main house at Travellers Rest began as a two-story, four-room house with hand-hewn logs and hand-formed shingles. Additions to the home were made over the years, and slave cabins and a carriage house were built. Major expansion came after 1820, when, at age fifty-four, Overton married Mrs. Mary McConnell (White) May, widow of Dr. Francis May. The widow May had five children. She was the daughter of Knoxville's founder, Brig. Gen. James White, and the sister of U.S.

Congressman Hugh Lawson White. John and Mary Overton had three more children: John Overton Jr. (1821–1898), Annie Coleman Overton Brinkley (1823–1845), and Elizabeth B. Overton Lea (1826–1890). Judge John Overton died at Travellers Rest on April 12, 1833.

On December 31, 1829, the State Legislature approved the incorporation of the Franklin Turnpike Company, authorizing it to sell shares toward the building of a turnpike from downtown Nashville to downtown Franklin. The Franklin Turnpike bisected the Travellers Rest property so that there came to be Overton property on both the east and the west sides of the pike. All the owners whose property it went through had to give their approval, including Travellers Rest and nearby Glen Leven plantations. The pike was to be completed within seven years, so it may have been finished by 1837. The first turnpike in the Nashville area, its ultimate cost was about $75,000. It had four tollgates; one was at the Hogan Road intersection of Franklin Pike. The home of First Presbyterian Church member Admiral Jerry Breast now includes the toll house, which was at Hogan Road. When it was no longer needed for tolls, it was moved eastward up the hill to its present location on Hogan Road.

Important Historical Occurrences at Travellers Rest

Remarkably significant things happened at Travellers Rest. Perhaps the two most notable would be the coordination of Andrew Jackson's 1824 campaign for President of the United States and the use of the estate as Confederate Headquarters prior to the 1864 Battle of Nashville.

Judge John Overton and Andrew Jackson were good friends, as has been stated, beginning with their lodging together in 1789 at the home of the widow of John Donelson. As Overton put it, "We commenced our career together; we slept, ate, and suffered together."[14] Of these friends, Frances Clifton summarizes:

> These two men, so different in temperament and in other personal traits, were nevertheless bound together in a friendship which continued uninterrupted from early manhood until Overton's death. Overton was among the chief promoters of Jackson's political aspirations,

and probably, none of Jackson's unofficial advisors had as much influence with him as did John Overton. As President, Jackson relied much upon Overton's advice on matters of state. Beyond question the President felt a deep personal loss upon the death of his long-time friend and associate."[15]

Travellers Rest, it is argued, served as the planning headquarters for Jackson's 1824 campaign for the U.S. Presidency, which he lost to John Quincy Adams. "Jackson's biographers agree that his presidential campaign was directed from Travellers Rest. Here the 'Nashville Junto'—Overton, William B. Lewis, John H. Eaton, and a few other Tennessee politicians—planned the maneuvers which put Old Hickory in the White House."[16] We wish there were more stories about those meetings. "However, much of the evidence which might have made Overton's role clearer was lost when, just before his death, he burned most of his correspondence with Jackson."[17] Overton was instrumental, as well, in the 1828 campaign. He was Chairman of the Nashville Committee for Jackson.[18]

It might be that Overton's greatest gift to his friend could be "his masterful handling of the 1827 attack on the legality of Jackson's marriage to Rachel Donelson Robards. Overton led the committee that collected a mass of material refuting the charge that the Jacksons had been guilty of adultery."[19]

Overton promised to visit Jackson in the White House annually and very nearly accomplished this. On a visit in 1831, they vacationed at the Virginia seashore village of Rip Rap. The lifetime friendship was very important to Jackson. A letter from mutual friend Ralph E. W. Earl to Overton, written in December 1831, illustrates:

> The President speaks often of you; nothing seems to give him more satisfaction than to receive a letter from his old and well-tried friend of Travellers Rest. I hope you will not disappoint us in your annual visit to Washington. It is not only gratifying to the President, but it is also to the rest of your friends and acquaintances here.[20]

Overton and the Creation of Memphis

Before the Jackson-Overton friendship is left behind, it is appropriate to make a brief mention of the Memphis story. It is not related to Travellers Rest or the church property we are studying per se; however, it shows how widespread Judge John Overton's influence actually was.

Before the judge worked on creating his estate south of Nashville, the young Overton used his law, surveying, and land speculation skills to acquire property in Tennessee. In 1794–1795, Overton purchased several large tracts of land in the Western District of North Carolina, land west of the Tennessee River that had been set aside by treaty as Chickasaw territory. These tracts, about 65,000 acres' worth, were the Rice grant property, purchased in 1783 by John Rice. Overton, in several installments, was able to buy these lands for what averaged out to be less than fifteen cents per acre.[21] Andrew Jackson was induced to participate i n a minor way in these purchases, gaining partial interest in the lands.

The land included several high bluffs along the Mississippi River. One tract of 5,000 acres was known as the fourth Chickasaw bluff, looking directly out onto the river. Upon this bluff area, John Overton created the town of Memphis, so named by a Mr. Winchester, another partner in the land business. As Memphis of the mighty Nile River was a major city, the developers intended to create a major city on the New World's mightiest river. The action of creating the town, laying out the streets and lots, and moving forward with the sale of lots, came only days after the 1818 treaty by which the Chickasaw tribe gave up their claims within the Western District. Tradition favors the thought that Overton, in his dealings for Western District and Mississippi River lands, sensed that hitching himself to the rising star of Andrew Jackson would be a wise move. As it turned out, it was Andrew Jackson who persuaded the Chickasaws to relinquish their lands.[22]

The tale of John Overton and Memphis is longer and more complex than can be told in the present volume; however, it is a valuable piece of the story of who Judge John Overton was.

John Overton Jr.

Judge John Overton died on April 12, 1833, at Travellers Rest. At that time, the estate covered about 2,300 acres. Control passed to his widow, Mary McConnell White Overton. His eldest son, John Overton Jr., was twelve at that time. Mary died in 1862, leaving Travellers Rest to John Jr., who would come to be known as Col. John Overton. He had married Rachel Harding, daughter of Thomas Harding, in 1841; she

Judge John Overton's son, Col. John Overton with wife Harriet Virginia Maxwell Overton. Courtesy of Travellers Rest Historic House Museum, Inc.

died in 1844. Thomas Harding was a member of First Presbyterian Church; ironically, in his family was a Harpeth River estate named Oak Hill. Six years later, John Overton Jr. married Harriet Virginia Maxwell, daughter of his neighbor, Jesse Maxwell Jr. Thus, Land Grant #367, arranged for by Jesse Maxwell Sr. in 1783, found itself again connected to that family. That connection will not be the last instance of the land grant becoming connected through marriage to significant families in this south-of-Nashville neighborhood.

John Overton Jr.'s 1862 assumption of leadership duties at Travellers Rest begins another era of great significance. Like his father, the young John had become well-known in business, civic affairs, and social circles. In addition, he was a justice of the peace and a state legislator. The attractive gardens around the house, the straight driveway (resembling Belle Meade Plantation and Jackson's Hermitage), and other aspects of the layout of Travellers Rest were products of Overton's vision.[23] The Overtons were all members of First Presbyterian Church, then at its downtown location at Spring and Summer streets (now 5th Avenue and Church Street).

Travellers Rest During the Civil War

The Civil War had begun by the time John Overton Jr. assumed the operation of the estate; however, it had little effect until Nashville was taken over and occupied by Federal troops on February 25, 1862. Overton did not favor Tennessee's secession from the Union (June 8, 1861, the 8th and final state to secede); however, he felt duty-bound to accept the responsibility offered him as commander of a regiment of militia. Upon the February occupation, Overton was advised to flee southward with his wife. He returned in 1864, just before the December Battle of Nashville.

The house at Travellers Rest, amazingly enough, was never seriously damaged during the war. A short time after the Battle of Franklin, John Bell Hood, the Confederate commander of the Army of Tennessee, chose Travellers Rest as his headquarters for the impending attempt to retake Nashville for the South. During the thirteen days of Travellers Rest as headquarters, it was noted that Mrs. Overton served dinner to seven Confederate generals: John Bell Hood; Benjamin F. Cheatham; Nathan Bedford Forrest; Stephen B. Lee; Edmund W. Pettus; W. H. Jackson; and James R. Chalmers.[24] The names of some of the seven have faded away, but a few did not. Nathan Bedford Forrest became a Grand Wizard of the Ku Klux Klan for a time after the war; his controversial bust was removed from the Tennessee State Capitol in July 2021. W. H. Jackson married into the Harding family of Belle Meade Plantation and co-managed the estate. Stephen D. Lee became the first President of Mississippi State University. James R. Chalmers was elected to Congress in Mississippi. The name of Edmund W. Pettus was attached to a bridge in Alabama after the war and, in 1965, became famous for a pivotal civil rights confrontation known as "Bloody Sunday."[25]

The Battle of Nashville took place on December 15–16, 1864. Since the battle lines for both days of the battle were not far away, it is deceptively easy to imagine that the church property was dotted with campsites and campfires of Confederates, chatting with comrades as they awaited instructions for the coming re-engagement with Federal forces. However, the realities of those days and nights are far from peaceful and calm.[26] The Battle of Nashville followed on the heels of the Battle of Franklin (November 30), a disaster for the Confederate Army of Tennessee. General John Bell Hood commanded the Army of Tennessee, supported by Lt. Gen. Alexander P. Stewart; Lt. Gen. Stephen D. Lee; Maj. Gen. Benjamin F. Cheatham; and Maj. Gen. Nathan Bedford Forrest. Union troops at Franklin were commanded by Gen. John M. Schofield, who retreated back to Nashville after Franklin. General George H. Thomas commanded the occupation forces in Nashville.

The Union army's move from Franklin to Nashville would have been characterized by thousands of troops walking on Franklin Pike; further, there would have been hundreds of wagons pulled by horses and mules driven by teamsters. The wagons were full of food supplies, wounded men, ammunition, and other supplies. Downtown Nashville had Union steamboats and warehouses waiting to re-supply the troops and handle the casualties. The First Presbyterian Church, then located at Spring and Summer Streets (now at the corner of 5th Avenue and

Church Street), was one of many Federal hospitals downtown. Days after the Union troops crossed the property on Franklin Pike, the Confederates came along. They were in terrible shape after the Franklin slaughter yet had no time to relax at a campsite. Fortifications had to be built along predicted battle lines, and the inclement weather was a great hindrance. Supplies were meager; soldiers were eating parched corn, and many were barefoot.

General Hood set himself up in a headquarters at the Overton Travellers Rest. After this, the future church property would have witnessed many couriers on horseback, traveling from Travellers Rest to commanders at dozens of locations along battle lines. The battle line for the first day's fighting generally stretched from Hillsboro Pike and along Woodmont Boulevard, all the way to Nolensville Pike. After a Confederate retreat, the second day's action was along what is now

Gen. Robert Bogardus Snowden and Col. John Overton are pictured above at an 1895 Confederate reunion in Memphis. Van Leer Kirkman's Oak Hill property was created when he bought land from each man in 1887. From *Confederate Magazine* 3, no. 6, June 1895. 186. Courtesy of Metro Nashville Archives.

Battery Lane, Harding Place, the I-65 interchange area, and over to Nolensville Pike.

A considerably important struggle happened at Peach Orchard Hill, the Travellers Rest peach grove area. This area is now the north end of Franklin Road Academy, overlooking Harding Place. It was in this battle that the Union Army's 13th Regiment of the U.S. Colored Infantry distinguished itself in a famous charge. Tradition holds that the Battle of Peach Orchard Hill was so fierce that the hill was completely blue with fallen Union soldiers. There is an excellent likelihood that the headquarters tent for Confederate General Stephen D. Lee was placed very near the northeast corner of today's Cheek House, out in the parking lot. From that high spot, through binoculars, there would have been a clear visual of the battle taking place at the peach orchard. In those days, there were no trees within miles of Nashville, all trees having been felled for buildings, fortifications, and firewood.

Someone walking on today's church property on December 16 would have heard the relentless noise of cannon fire. At one point, one or more cannons were hastily rolled to what is now the corner of Franklin Pike and Tyne Boulevard; a historical marker a few yards away on Tyne Boulevard tells the story of a skirmish at that spot. There came a time on December 16 when Confederate forces were finally routed at Shy's Hill (then Compton's Hill), at the peach orchard, and all along the battle line. The battle went to the Union side as the Confederates were routed. Indeed, it was a panic. The Confederate forces literally threw down their weapons and ran south down Granny White Pike and Franklin Pike, including church property, chased by the Union troops. In a memoir, a rueful John Bell Hood said that he "beheld for the first and only time a Confederate Army abandon the field in confusion."[27]

The Confederate retreat went all the way south to Alabama, chased by Union soldiers for days afterward. Soldiers by the thousands would flee across future First Presbyterian Church acres. It was said that it took four days to find and bury the dead and gather discarded weapons and gear.[28] This hasty retreat provided future souvenir hunters with metal detectors with a fertile ground for discovery. Even in modern times, artifact hunters are sure to come around when the church has had occasion for digging.

Col. John Overton eventually got most of his property back after the war. However, all the land had been ravaged by soldiers camping, cutting trees for firewood, foraging for food, and all the other ways armies and battles damage property.

Overton Property Parceled Out

On April 25, 1887, Colonel Overton sold a 64-acre (exactly "64 and 408/1000"!) section of the original 640-acre Land Grant #367 to wealthy Nashville businessman Van Leer Kirkman for $12,881.[29] This tract would become the home of First Presbyterian Church of Nashville. The Kirkman purchase will be examined further in the next chapter.

Colonel John Overton died on December 12, 1898. The Travellers Rest property upon which the house and immediate grounds sat passed to Harriet Overton. The rest of the vast property was apportioned to the Overton children. Harriet died in 1899, and the central estate was passed to her son, May Overton.

By 1930, Travellers Rest, then owned by Judge Overton's great-grandson Jacob McGavock Dickinson, had become the largest and best-known Arabian horse farm in the United States. In 1946, Dickinson sold Travellers Rest to Nashville physician Dr. John B. Youmans. The Louisville and Nashville Railroad (L&N) bought the property in 1951. In 1954, the L&N gave the three acres the house sits on to the National Society of Colonial Dames in America. A restoration was begun in 1964 under the leadership of Mrs. Andrew Benedict Jr., and the home was eventually restored to an 1820–1830 configuration and decoration. It continues as a museum, an archaeological site, and a wedding venue.[30]

Through the years after Colonel Overton died, Travellers Rest was parceled out by inheritance and sales outside the family. All Overton lands, presumably as desired by Overton himself, carried restrictions that "ran with the land." We might today call them covenants. These restrictions are typically prohibitions against "shops, stores, factories, asylums, hospitals, charitable institutions, and schools." No swine were allowed. Only residences could be built, and they were restricted as to size and placement on lots. And no persons "of African descent" could buy or lease these lands but could live on them if they were servants.[31] These kinds of restrictions are found on deed after deed all over this neighborhood, presumably effective until unenforceable or, indeed, illegal, and certainly had their effect on the future City of Oak Hill.

Chapter Three

Van Leer Kirkman's Purchase and Era: 1887–1923

The First Presbyterian Church property at 4815 Franklin Road began to take its present shape in 1887 when wealthy Nashville businessman Van Leer Kirkman purchased "64 and 408/1000 acres" of Travellers Rest estate land from Col. John Overton and Harriet Virginia Overton. Both names are on the April 25, 1887, court document. The acreage was one-tenth of the 640-acre Land Grant #367, which Judge John Overton had bought from William and Moses Maxwell. Kirkman paid $12,881.60 for this land.[1]

The tract in this 1887 purchase fronted the Franklin Turnpike, as it was known. The Franklin Pike frontage is the same today as it was at that time. Neither Robertson Academy Road nor Tyne Boulevard existed then; the sixty-four acres were simply carved out of larger Overton lands. The far western end of the tract was about where Churchwood Lane now runs. In those days, what was called a turnpike was little more than a wide wagon path with a gravel mix instead of dirt.

Kirkman had previously purchased a considerably larger adjoining tract on April 2, 1887, from Robert B. and Annie Overton Snowden of Shelby County, Tennessee. This tract, which included portions of Land Grant #60 (Samuel Barton) and Land Grant #390 (Archibald Lytle), was 282 acres and was purchased for $35,250.[2] This Snowden land itself was previously part of Travellers Rest, too. Judge John Overton

---

Opposite page: Picture of Van Leer Kirkman on Nashville periodical *Chat* 3, no. 21, April 1895. Courtesy of Tennessee State Library and Archives.

General Road Map of
DAVIDSON COUNTY
TENNESSEE
14
10
12
11
13
8
3
4
2
7
9
16
5

GLENDALE PARK
GLENWOOD
GLENDALE ROAD
SIX
PIKE
7
10
BATTERY LANE
KIRKMAN ROAD
COMPTON RD.
WHITE PIKE
BLVD
FRANKLIN PIKE
OTTER CR RD.
RADNOR LAKE
HOGAN

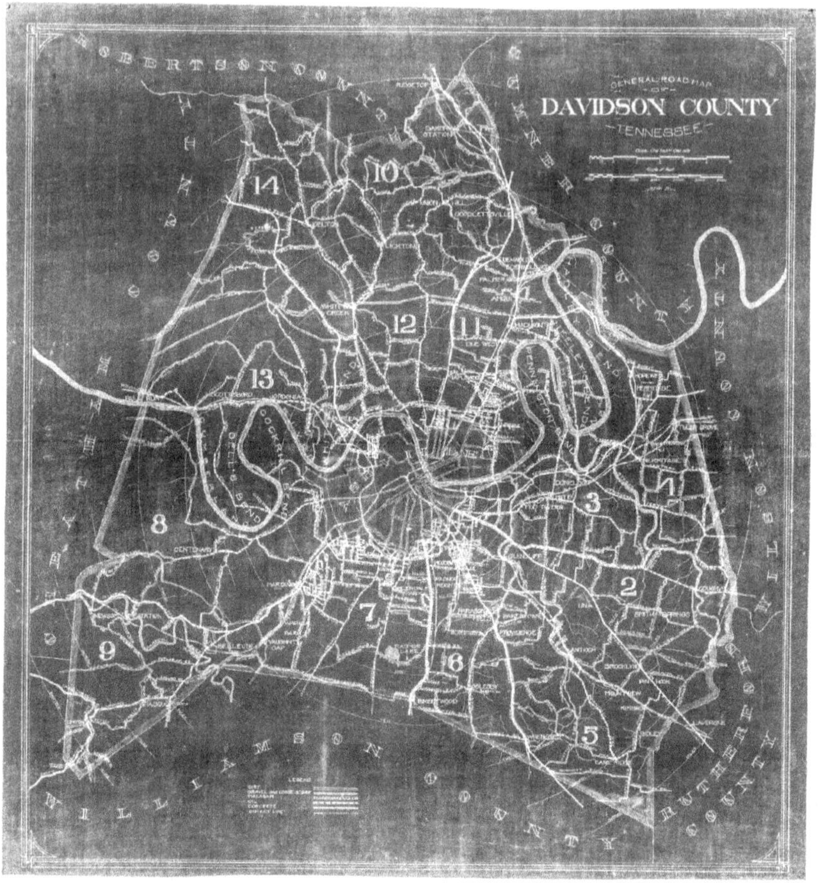

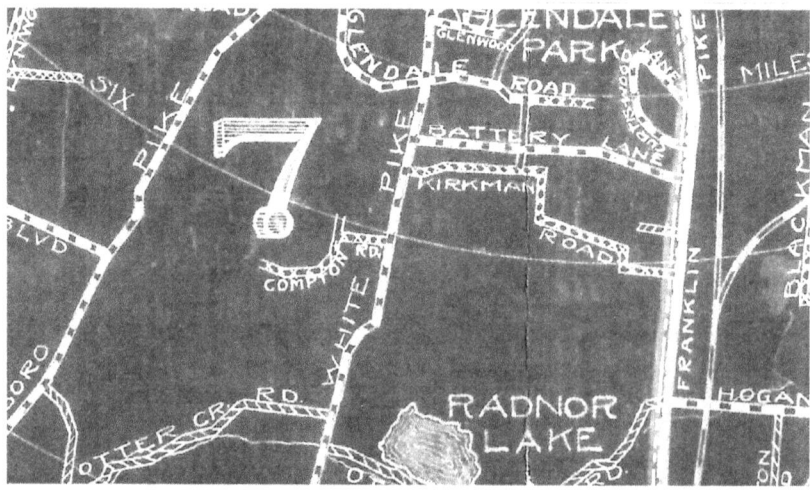

had purchased the 640-acre Barton grant in 1799 and 159 acres of the Lytle grant in 1830.³ Annie Overton Brinkley Snowden was the granddaughter of Judge Overton and Mary M. White Overton. Col. Robert Bogardus Snowden distinguished himself in the Confederate Army. The Snowden purchase gave Kirkman a tract of land which extended westward almost to what is now Lealand Lane and northward to what is now Glendale Lane.

Van Leer Kirkman

Van Leer Kirkman was a native Nashvillian who became one of its leading businessmen. He was born on March 25, 1849, to Hugh and Eleanora Chambers Van Leer Kirkman. The Kirkman house was a mansion at the corner of the then Cedar and Summer Streets, now Charlotte Pike and 5th Avenue, across the street from St. Mary's Cathedral. Hugh and Eleanora moved into that house the day before Van Leer was born in it. His mother never left the house, succumbing two months later due to complications of the birth. That old house at Charlotte and 5th Avenue later became Ward Seminary, then Nashville Music Conservatory, and, at one time, was used for a Federal Court.⁴ In 1915, the State Senate met there. In 1900, apparently, Mrs. Van Leer Kirkman (Kate) had sold the house to the company that became Washington Manufacturing Company. By 1930, the house had been torn down. The lot eventually became part of the Andrew Jackson Office Building.⁵

Hugh Kirkman, Van Leer's father, stayed in the home until his 1861 death when Van Leer was about twelve. Hugh had sent his daughter, Mary Florence Kirkman, to boarding school in New York and taken Van Leer to Cumberland Furnace, Tennessee, "to be brought up in the home of adoring grandfather A. W. [Anthony Wayne] Van Leer."⁶ Young Van Leer Kirkman joined the Confederate Army when he was

---

Opposite page: This 1910 (?) map of Davidson County shows how Kirkman Road (also known as Kirkman Lane and later the Bridle Path) connected Travellers Rest with the Lealand property on Granny White Pike. Note that there is no Tyne Blvd. yet; the short Compton Lane will become part of Tyne Blvd. Courtesy of Tennessee State Library and Archives.

fourteen, serving first under Col. Thomas G. Woodward and then under General Nathan Bedford Forrest. When A. W. Van Leer died in 1864, he left a great fortune to his heirs from highly profitable iron works in Dickson County, including 20,000 acres of land in that area. There is still a small town north of Dickson, Tennessee, called Vanleer.

First Marriage and Family Controversy

Kirkman married his first wife, Samuella Berry, on August 4, 1868. She was the daughter of well-known Nashville bookseller William T. Berry. Van Leer and Samuella's children were Ella Kirkman, who married Bruce Douglas, whose family name is preserved by the Douglas Corner area of 8th Avenue South, and Hugh Clark Kirkman, who married Louise Bransford, daughter of William Bransford. Samuella died on November 12 or 13, 1880, when she was only thirty. Her cause of death is not mentioned in any news account. An unknown newspaper writer wrote a touching column after noting her passing in "recent obituary notices.":

> It may not be out of place to say that as her life was gentle, and
> Singularly free from ostentation and obtrusiveness, her last
> Moments were those of perfect resignation and repose, so quiet
> And so free from pain that one hardly knew when she breathed her last—a beautiful translation.
> —A silent sufferer for many months, it is believed that no expression of impatience or forgetfulness ever escaped her lips—'a soft, meek, patient, tranquil spirit' marked her every word and act.[7]

Things must have been very interesting in the larger Kirkman family. Van Leer had a sister, Mary Florence, who caused quite a stir in Nashville in 1863 when she married a Union soldier from the occupying force in Nashville. Friends and relations alike shunned her, even refusing to attend her wedding. No one extended any courtesies at all except a neighbor, Mrs. Snowden, who gave her a reception. These are the Snowdens who owned property south of Nashville that would eventually be bought by Mary Florence's brother, Van Leer, in 1887. After the death of Mary Florence's grandfather, A. W. Van Leer, in 1864, her husband, a Captain Drouillard, resigned his commission in the Union Army to throw himself into the running of the iron works business in Cumberland Furnace.[8]

According to church records, Van Leer's father, Hugh Kirkman, was a member of First Presbyterian Church, as was the whole family of Samuella Berry Kirkman. So, we might assume that Van Leer was also of that congregation. However, his church affiliation changed after his second marriage, when Van Leer, his new wife, and their children all were members of Christ Church, the Episcopal Church in downtown Nashville.

Second Marriage—to a Socialite

Van Leer Kirkman's second marriage took place on December 30, 1886, in Memphis. His second bride was Katherine (Kate) Thompson of Oxford, Mississippi. Kate was the daughter of Caswell Macon Thompson, who built the first hotel in Oxford that was constructed after the Civil War, Thompson House. It was built on the site of the first hotel in Oxford, the Oxford Inn, located on the central square. Federal troops burned down the Oxford Inn in 1864; it was rebuilt in 1869–70. The Thompson House in Oxford has been brought back from disrepair in the modern era by the Tollison and Webb Law Firm, whose offices occupy the building.

Caswell Macon Thompson's father was Jacob Thompson, lawyer, Governor of Mississippi (1862–1864), and Congressman from Mississippi. Jacob was appointed Secretary of the Interior by President James Buchanan in 1857. He sided with the Confederacy when war broke out and was made a General. Jacob was present at battles in Vicksburg, Corinth, and Tupelo, Mississippi. He was also a Confederate spy in Canada toward the war's end. He settled in Memphis after the War and served on the Board of Trustees of the University of the South (Sewanee).[9]

All these Thompsons were kin to the Thompsons of Nashville's Glen Leven farm estate. The Nashville Thompsons were members of First Presbyterian Church. The Glen Leven home still stands on Franklin Road, north of Harding Place.[10]

With his inherited wealth, the young Van Leer Kirkman was at home in the most exclusive social and business circles in Nashville. Here is one description from a small Nashville periodical:

> Immediately after [the Civil War] he went to England and spent three years studying under a tutor. Mr. Kirkman is strikingly handsome in appearance and of splendid physique. He is a representative Southern gentleman, of characteristic cordiality and easy bearing. He lives at Oak Hill, one of the handsomest country places in the South, and there with his charming wife, the former Katherine Thompson of Memphis, dispenses a generous hospitality. Mr. Kirkman is an ardent lover of the thoroughbred … is President of the Cumberland Park Racing Association, is a director of many of the city's substantial corporations, and was for many years President of the Hermitage Club.[11]

The young Kate Thompson was wealthy and well-connected in her own right. In an excerpt from a national magazine in 1897, she was described as follows:

> A conspicuous figure in Southern society is Mrs. Van Leer Kirkman of Nashville, President of the Woman's Board of the Tennessee Centennial Exposition. Though of striking appearance, beautiful and gracious, the daughter of an old and honored family, Mrs. Kirkman's prominence comes chiefly from her cultural attainments, and her place on the Board of Exposition Managers is wholly due to her executive ability.
>
> From the hour of her debut in Memphis, Katherine Thompson was an acknowledged Belle throughout the South. At White Sulphur and Old Point, In the Carolinas in summer and Florida and New Orleans in winter, her beauty and accomplishments made her popular. She

became the wife of Van Leer Kirkman, a prominent son of Tennessee, in 1886, and now lives at Oak Hill, five miles from Nashville. Her home is as famous for its hospitality as the land about it is known for its blue grass.

Mrs. Kirkman is the daughter of C. M. Thompson, only son of the late Jacob Thompson, Secretary of the Interior under President Buchanan, and afterward a member of the cabinet of the Confederate States. As a girl she spent four years in Cuba with her grandparents. Returning to Memphis, she began her education with the Episcopal Sisters of St. Mary. Her studies were continued at Fairmount College, and at 16 she went abroad—to school in Paris and to travel.[12]

The December 30, 1886, wedding of Van Leer Kirkman and Katherine Thompson was quite the winter social event of that year. One of Nashville's newspapers made note of the many Nashvillians who would be riding the train to Memphis for the festivities. They included bridesmaid Ella Kirkman, Van Leer's daughter by Samuella Berry Kirkman; Captain and Mrs. J. P. Drouillard [this is Mary Florence, the Kirkman sister who married the Union officer during the War]; Miss Hensley; Miss Mamie Vaughn; Mr. and Mrs. Hugh Craighead; Mr. and Mrs. John Overton; Mr. Jo Thompson; Mr. Clark Pritchett, Miss Pritchett, Mr. Van Pritchett, Sam Pritchett Sr.; Miss Lizzie Ewing; Miss Fannie Ray McAlister; Mr. John Demoville; Miss Mamie Taylor; Capt. Joe Phillips; Messrs. John Thompson, May Overton, Van Polk, Matt Gardner, R. T. Kirkpatrick, Bruce Douglas, Norman Kirkman, Major Jo Lockhart, Chas. D. Porter, Frank Fogg; and guests from Frankfort, KY and Ohio.[13]

The day of the wedding was miserably cold and wet. One's imagination in the modern day can easily see the humor in the proceedings; the actuality was probably not funny at all. A 2017 summary by the Executive Director of the Tennessee Historical Society uses Memphis newspaper accounts to bring it all alive:

'No social event in recent years has excited public interest to so intense a pitch as the wedding of Miss

Kate Thompson to Mr. Van Leer Kirkman,' declared the Memphis Daily Appeal society editor on December 31, 1886. What can be more exciting than a New Year's party? The New Year's wedding of 'the catch of the State' and 'the acknowledged belle of Memphis.' Newspapers in Memphis, Nashville, and Little Rock covered the wedding. It was on Thursday December 30, 1886, at Calvary Episcopal Church, in downtown Memphis. Over 1,000 guests filled every spot in the church; two policemen on duty 'were immediately overwhelmed' by 'the dense crowd' when the doors were at last opened. Outside, the weather was a freezing drizzle, and the streets were a muddy mess. Nuns of St Mary's School, where Kate had been a student, decorated the church with flowers. Eight couples of bridesmaids and groomsmen were in the party, each bridesmaid carrying bouquets of Duchess of Brabant roses, tied with pink ribbons. Her cousin West J. Crawford led her down the aisle. Kate, 22, was noted as 'one of the most beautiful women in Tennessee.' The groom was wealthy, widowed, and 37. The couple went first to a reception at the mansion of the bride's grandmother, the wealthy Catherine Jones Thompson. One room, devoted to the exhibition of 'costly presents' of 'wide variety,' included 'the complete silver service of 110 pieces,' which Mrs. Thompson gave to her granddaughter. Guests then went to a New Year's party at the Memphis Merchants' Exchange at the Cotton Exchange Building. The popular Arnold's Band played until the wee hours as 500 revelers danced. Kate entered the marriage with a dowry including an annual income of $1,000 and a $10,000 gift from her grandmother. She and her sister were also heirs to the considerable estate of her grandparents—her recently deceased grandfather, Jacob Thompson, was a millionaire. Van Leer Kirkman was heir to a fortune that included ironworks in Dickson County and lived on his investments. In 1887, the wealthy newlyweds built a mansion on their estate and thoroughbred farm, Oak Hill, south of Nashville on

Franklin Pike. They had 3 sons: Van Leer Kirkman, Jr. (1887), Caswell Macon Thompson Kirkman (1889), and Anthony Wayne Kirkman (1893).[14]

Toplovich's entertaining summary of the newspaper accounts notes that the gathered press covered almost every aspect of the spectacle of this wedding:

> When the groom's party of more than 40 Nashvillians arrived, they were unable to move through the mass for 20 minutes—one lady in the group fainted from the press. The bride and her attendants had problems, too standing in the weather 'for five minutes exposed to wet hair and the peril of the rush.' The bride was noted as '... a picture of unsurpassing loveliness.' Her gown was 'white moiré en train, with white tulle overskirt,' with a veil of white tulle and orange blossoms. 'An involuntary exclamation' from 'a thousand pairs of cherry lips' rose in the air at the vision of the bride. The groom ... was declared 'as far as manly beauty goes, a fit mate for the superb woman he has won ... as fine a specimen of physical manhood as one will see in a day's travel.' As the couple moved out of the chancel [with] the organ playing the grand march from Wagner's Tannhäuser, 'an involuntary sigh ran through the audience as the fair vision faded out of sight.'[15]

The Move to Franklin Pike

For the six years before this wedding, Van Leer Kirkman had been a widower, living in the 8th Avenue/Douglas Avenue home that had been his with his first wife, Samuella. The 1886 wedding to Kate Thompson began an extremely eventful span of years in Kirkman's life. The first thing on the agenda of the new couple seems to have been a decision to buy some property and move farther south of Nashville. In 1887, the Kirkmans bought from Annie Overton Brinkley Snowden and Robert Snowden 282 acres of land, part of Land Grant #60 (the Barton grant) that Judge John Overton himself had bought by 1829.

Annie Overton Brinkley Snowden was the Judge's granddaughter. Also in 1887, Kirkman bought 64-plus acres on the Franklin Turnpike from Col. John Overton. These acres abutted the eastern side of the Snowden purchase, giving the Kirkmans about 346 acres of land, all, originally, Overton land. They built a showcase mansion on the Franklin Pike part of the land, right about where today's Cheek House and Columbarium of First Presbyterian Church of Nashville are located. There were other buildings, too; however, we can no longer pinpoint what or where they were.

What precipitated the Kirkmans' move to the Franklin Pike location? We can only guess in the absence of any memoirs or writings of any kind. Three possibilities present themselves.

1. A new start for a new couple. It seems natural and logical that Van Leer and Kate would desire a place that did not have the memories associated with his first wife, Samuella.

2. A memoir associated with the Thompson family of Franklin Pike mentions the Kirkmans in an interesting way. Mary Hamilton Thompson Orr, a granddaughter of Col. John Overton, suggests that her grandmother, Harriet Virginia Maxwell Overton, admired the new Mrs. Kirkman and wished for her to move from the 8th Avenue/Douglas Avenue neighborhood to Franklin Pike, not far from Glen Leven, the home and property of the Thompson family. These Thompsons were distantly related to Kate Thompson Kirkman. Mrs. Orr, when she was quite old, was interviewed by nephew Joe (Tiger Joe) Thompson. In the interview, Mrs. Orr gives her interesting take on the Kirkman move:

> My grandmother Overton was a lady of her own mind, and had notions. She was very much impressed by Mrs. Van Leer Kirkman, who had married Van Leer Kirkman, whose people owned down here at Douglas Avenue. She [Mrs. Kirkman] wanted a place farther in the country, and grandmother wanted her out there. [She] made grandfather [Col. Overton] sell her Oak Hill, which was mother's. He had set that aside for my mother.[16]

3. An interesting notion is that Kirkman could have been allowed to purchase the sixty-four-plus acres from Col. John Overton as part of the agreement in 1887 that saw Kirkman become President of a new horse-breeding enterprise in the neighborhood, known as the "Hermitage Stud."[17] This new business specialized in breeding, training, racing, and selling trotting horses. In 1886, brothers May Overton, Jesse Maxwell Overton, and Robert L. Overton, sons of Colonel Overton, and son-in-law John Overton, bought some horses in Kentucky. They decided to create a stud business, persuading Nashville businessman Van Leer Kirkman to head up the business as President. (Robert Overton actually succeeded his brother-in-law Hugh Craighead as one of the original officers.)

The Hermitage Stud Enterprise and Other Business Deals

The Hermitage Stud property was on both sides of Franklin Pike. It went from Kirkman's Oak Hill on the South to Curtiswood Lane on the North. All the land was Overton land; Oak Hill itself was not part of the stud farm. All the buildings but one and the oval training track were west of Franklin Pike. The land for the stud operation was destined to be inherited by the Overton children. Each child knew ahead of Colonel Overton's death which part of the Travellers Rest property was to be inherited by him or her. The land-owners-to-be decided to use their designated land for the new money-making project. Nearly all of the Hermitage Stud enterprise was located on land that would be inherited by Mary McConnell Overton Thompson (Mrs. John Thompson). The extensive training track ran north-south from where Battery Lane is now to the South Curtiswood Lane area and includes the modern-day Hazelwood Lane neighborhood. The Hermitage Stud office building is the only structure still left and is located in a family's backyard on South Curtiswood Lane.

Hermitage Stud did well enough as a business; however, there eventually were financial problems, including a bank-closing panic in 1893. There came a time when the issues were too great, and the Hermitage Stud closed in 1898, the same year Col. John Overton died. William Gerst bought the business and eventually moved it to a different property. In about 1908, the Pawnee Bill Circus wintered on the Hermitage Stud site, complete with camels and a rhinoceros. By 1910, Battery Lane had been established through the Hermitage Stud property. Soon after that, Mary McConnell Overton Thompson donated several of the southernmost acres bordering Kirkman land to the Trustees of Robertson Academy for the purpose of moving the school to the property and building new buildings.[18]

Before the Robertson Academy donation of land, Mrs. Thompson, in 1910, sold 4.87 acres of Franklin Pike-facing land to Robert F. Jones. The property was between Franklin Pike and the acres that became Robertson Academy. Robertson Academy itself was built next to the Jones house. This story is told in Chapter Seven under the subheading: "The Sumner Property."

Van Leer Kirkman was involved in yet another late 1880s business deal when, in 1887, he sold 250 acres of land south of Nashville to a syndicate of business, real estate, and transportation leaders. This land was not part of his Overton land but, instead, was the land he had owned and lived on during his marriage to Samuella Berry Kirkman. In his book, *Recollections of a Lifetime*, wealthy Nashville businessman James E. Caldwell says he had to form a syndicate to buy 250 acres of land from Van Leer Kirkman to obtain a right-of-way for a streetcar line to go to his Glendale Park project. The purchase from Kirkman was eventually subdivided and became the Nashville suburb Waverly on both sides of Franklin Pike, south of the city reservoir.[19] Several of the syndicate members, including James E. Caldwell and Percy Warner, were First Presbyterian Church members.

Kirkman had all this land because, by 1887, he had, through "conveyances and maneuverings," acquired from a syndicate the home and considerable agrarian land of "Belle Vue," a former plantation in the area. The Belle Vue home had been the home of William T. Berry, Samuella's father, and had become the marital home of Van Leer and Samuella Kirkman.[20]

One of the Cars on the Nashville & Franklin Interurban Railway. Caught by the Camera at the Custom House Corner.

The Nashville-Franklin Interurban Railway daily passed by both the Kirkman and the Cheek versions of "Oak Hill," from 1909–1942. Picture from *Nashville Banner*, May 22, 1909. Courtesy of Metro Nashville Archives.

The Kirkman stop still sits on Franklin Road at what is now an entrance to Franklin Road Academy. Photo by author, 2022.

Kirkman's Oak Hill. Van Leer Kirkman and sons pictured far right. Courtesy of Tennessee State Library and Archives.

Entrance to Van Leer Kirkman's Oak Hill Estate, circa 1900. Courtesy of Tennessee State Library and Archives.

Oak Hill and the Centennial Exposition

Van Leer and Katherine's Oak Hill was a place of grandeur and splendor. It became a location for Nashville society gatherings. An 1887 newspaper article noted that the editor of Turf, *Field and Farm* magazine had recently enjoyed the ride out Franklin Pike with Kirkman for a visit to the property. His take on Oak Hill:

> Mr. Kirkman is building a new house on what he has christened Oak Hill, and in planting his garden he turned to the surface 24 shells and cannon balls. The lawn of 35 acres in front of the house is shaded by oak and sugar trees, and to the rear rise, in picturesque grandeur, the Overton Hills, the outpost of the Harpeth Hills. It is a charming spot, clothed in the verdure of Peace, and Mr. Kirkman is constructing a home which will last for all time.[21]

Described elsewhere as "a palatial residence," it was noted that the house was built with Kate's money; the title was in her name. This "proved to be fortuitous because Mr. Kirkman was a clubman, turfman and racehorse breeder, vocations from which the monetary outgo proved considerably greater than the income."[22]

It may be that the Kirkmans' Oak Hill estate became Tennessee's most well-known society place in 1897, the year of the Tennessee Centennial Exposition. Both Van Leer and Kate were heavily involved in this significant event. Van Leer was the first Vice-President of the Exposition, while Kate was President of the Woman's Board. Her role turned out to be far more influential than anyone expected. The Woman's Board consisted of 100 women from across Tennessee, assisted by 320 women "commissioners." During the six-month run of the Exposition, Kate Kirkman gave almost weekly receptions at Oak Hill and was considered "Nashville's most famous hostess of the day."[23]

One of those gala receptions during the Exposition saw the Kirkmans hosting the United Confederate Veterans on June 25, 1897. This likely was in conjunction with a Confederate veterans' celebration at the Exposition, for Oak Hill was being prepared for the veterans and their sponsors, maids of honor, and friends. The newspaper, the day before the Kirkman gathering, noted that the estate was part of the Battle of Nashville battlefield. Both Van Leer and Kate were avid supporters of the Confederacy. He was a member of General Forrest's staff, "and a more loyal Confederate would be difficult to find." The front lawn of Oak Hill featured piles of cannon balls dug from estate grounds. Mrs. Kirkman prepared a "Confederates' Corner," which was her "especial pride." General Joseph Wheeler and daughter, relatives of Mrs. Kirkman, were to be guests, as was Mrs. Semmes-Colston of Mobile, Alabama, daughter of Admiral Raphael Semmes.[24]

It is very likely that the Confederate Corner of the house—an indoor display?—would have had some letters or mementos about Jefferson Davis' daughter, Varina Anne, since Katherine Thompson was friends with her at Fairmount Female College in Monteagle, Tennessee, in the 1880s.[25]

Kate Kirkman's Leadership and the Floral Parade

Kate Kirkman proved to be a strong leader for her women's department at the Tennessee Centennial Exposition. Accordingly, a day was set aside to honor her work. Kate Kirkman Day was September 30, 1897, and it was quite memorable. Though the visit of President and Mrs. McKinley to the Exposition earlier in its six-month run was special, it was said that the event "best remembered by spectators and participants" was the Floral Parade on Kate's day. It was called "the most superb effort the people of Nashville have ever made in the way of a display."[26] The Floral Parade was so spectacular that a standard history of Nashville devoted eight pages just to the parade itself, taken from the definitive book on the history of the Tennessee Centennial.

The parade began with a "Bicycle Division" of some twenty-two bicyclers dressed in white; floral decorations covered the bicycles. A marching band followed, then nearly 100 horse-drawn floats, wagons, carriages, "victorias, phaetons, and traps." Each was fully decorated with fresh flowers and accompanied by horse and rider escorts. Each conveyance was said to be "like a moving garden." Beautifully dressed young women adorned the floats amidst many flowers. The ultimate carriage

MRS. VAN LEER KIRKMAN,
PRESIDENT WOMAN'S BOARD TENNESSEE CENTENNIAL EXPOSITION.

Kate Thompson Kirkman, from *Official History of the Tennessee Centennial Celebration*; courtesy of Tennessee State Library and Archives.

was Kate Kirkman's, "literally covered in violets." Kate was dressed in a rose-colored *moiré* silk dress, covered in embroidered mousseline and lace. Her baby, Wayne, was by her side. Other flowers on her carriage had been supplied by the Nineteenth Century Club of Memphis, the State Federation of Women's Clubs, and the Daughters of the

American Revolution. The long parade wound around the Parthenon, Lake Watauga, and other streets and places on the Exposition grounds. Scores of women and girls were stationed along the way to toss flower petals of dozens of named species. The parade "passed and repassed, and, finally, every one of the untold thousands gathered to witness the parade had seen the carriages sufficiently."[27]

Kate Thompson Kirkman's ascendancy to the pinnacle of achievement and acclaim was not without some controversy. Her election to the Presidency of the Woman's Board in an 1896 meeting at the Maxwell House Hotel had been a surprise. Mrs. Hugh Craighead (the former Elizabeth Overton), a daughter of Col. John Overton, had resigned. She intended that her successor be Mrs. Leslie Warner. Board members, including Kate Kirkman, knew this, and the election of a successor was headed for a non-contested vote. But, in a most unusual turn of events, a behind-the-scenes campaign had materialized in support of Kate Kirkman. Her supporters had worked the Woman's Board rolls to bring absent board members' proxies to the election, and Mrs. John Hill Eakin nominated Kate Kirkman for President. Protests were lodged about the proxy votes; however, the general counsel of the Exposition gave approval for the absentee votes to count. Kate defeated Mrs. Warner. More protests followed, but the election was ultimately certified.[28]

Kate Kirkman's strong will guided the Woman's Department (also known as the Woman's Board) to spectacular success at the Exposition. However, her focus on a particular understanding of women in society was not universally accepted. Some women had wished for more emphasis on the emerging suffragette movement and less on home and flowers.[29]

Van Leer Kirkman, apparently from overwork during the Exposition, suffered a stroke. He lived but was an invalid for the next fourteen years until his 1911 death at Oak Hill. But the parties continued there, even in his invalid state. *The Nashville American* amply covered a typical party in 1910 in pictures and text:

> Oak Hill, in the zenith of its springtime beauty, was the scene yesterday … when Mr. and Mrs. Van Leer Kirkman

Woman's Building at 1897 Tennessee Centennial Celebration, from Official History of the Tennessee Centennial Exposition. Courtesy of Tennessee State Library and Archives.

Monument Honoring Kate Thompson Kirkman at Centennial Park on the site where the Woman's Pavilion stood. Photo by the author.

entertained their friends at a musical and garden tea. For a number of years this has been a feature of the spring scene eagerly anticipated by guests fortunate enough to have been invited.

The article described the giant oaks outside, pink hydrangeas, palms, and foliage. Inside were soft rose-colored walls of the drawing room where the Kirkmans greeted guests amid pink and white peonies by the thousands. Mr. Douglas Wright accompanied singers on the piano and offered vocal numbers himself. Guests received special gifts to remember the occasion: golden pins inscribed with "Oak Hill" and the date for the women and tie clasps for the men. Welcoming the guests, along with Mr. and Mrs. Kirkman, were Mr. and Mrs. Joseph H. Thompson; Mrs. William S. Bransford; Mrs. Harry W. Evans; Mrs. Thomas J. Tyne; Mrs. William P. Rutland; Mrs. J. S. Robinson; Mrs. Alex Caldwell; Miss Rebecca Polk; and Miss Katherine Berry.[30]

During the Kirkman years at Oak Hill, streetcar service between Nashville and Franklin began. The Nashville & Franklin Interurban Railway started its operation on May 1, 1909,[31] running until about 1940. The tracks were on the east side of Franklin Road as they passed Oak Hill. (Between Nashville and Franklin, there was some zigzagging from one side of the street to another.) A streetcar shelter still exists on the east side of the Robertson Academy Road intersection. Popular lore says that Van Leer Kirkman had the stop built himself; it was called Kirkman stop on one version of the schedule.

Van Leer Kirkman died at the Oak Hill residence on January 28, 1911. His obituary noted that his stroke and extended period of being an invalid stemmed from "overwork and worry" during the Centennial Exposition. It was also pointed out that he owned a great number of racehorses and was particularly known for guiding the development of both the West End Racing Park [now Centennial Park] and the Cumberland Park [now Fairgrounds] racetracks. The funeral was at Christ Church, Episcopal, in Nashville. Pallbearers were John W. Thomas; Joe Warner; Dr. Lucius Burch; Walter O. Palmer; W. L. Granbery; Thomas J. Tyne; George Washington; Richard Plater; and Ed Gardner.[32] An article a day later noted that "Tennessee [had] lost one of the most picturesque figures of the turf, and a man who had done as much as any other to make Tennessee thoroughbreds noted for excellence the world over."[33]

Kate continued to manage the Oak Hill estate, which had horses, cows, and crops. There was even a dairy operation, noted in the 1915 Nashville City Directory as "Oak Hill Dairy—Mrs. V. L. Kirkman—Franklin Pike." Society pages show that she visited relatives and friends around the country from time to time.

The Sale of Oak Hill

Twelve years after Van Leer Kirkman died, Kate sold the Oak Hill estate to W. H. Soper, a former Nashville resident who had been in the coal and iron business in West Virginia for many years. The selling price was $167,500. At the same time, she purchased the Edwin Warner home and one-half of the sixteen-acre estate in the "Richland addition" out Harding Road (West End Avenue.) The purchase price for "Elmington" was $55,000. Possession of each home was to happen on March 1, 1923. It was said that Soper would use the Oak Hill estate as his residence.[34]

The Warner home was located near the 8th and 9th holes of the Nashville Golf and Country Club, on the south side of Harding Pike. Edwin Warner was a charter member of the club; members decided it would be a good idea to build homes on the course. The Warner family suspects that the house burned during the Depression. One of Edwin and Susan's children was Susanne, who married attorney James O. Bass.[35] The Warners and the Basses were members of First Presbyterian Church.

Kate Kirkman died at her Harding Road home on March 3, 1926. With her at her death were Commander Van Leer Kirkman, Jr., USN, Washington, DC; Macon Kirkman, Helena, AR; Wayne Kirkman and Clark Kirkman. Wayne and Clark lived with her. Mrs. Bruce Douglas (Ella) was also there. Ella and Clark were Van Leer's children by his first wife, Samuella Berry.[36]

Van Leer Kirkman, Kate Thompson Kirkman, Samuella Berry Kirkman, Caswell Macon Thompson Kirkman, Anthony Wayne Van

Leer Kirkman, Ella Kirkman Douglas, and many other relatives are all buried in Mt. Olivet Cemetery in Nashville, in Section 3, around a tall Van Leer obelisk.[37]

This beautiful building is the residence of Mrs. Van Leer Kirkman. It consists of over three hundred acres. The Cumberland Presbyterians of this city are undertaking to purchase this property as a site for the proposed denominational school of the Cumberland Presbyterian church. An endowment of a half million dollars has already been procured for the school.

A planned sale of the Van Leer Kirkman property to the Cumberland Presbyterian denomination, as described in the photo, never happened. No further information on this interesting possibility has been discovered. From the *Nashville Banner*, April 23, 1922. Courtesy of Metro Nashville Archives.

CHAPTER FOUR

☦

Rogers Caldwell's Time: 1925–1929

The years of Rogers and Margaret Caldwell living at Oak Hill may be the least-known-about era in the history of the Franklin Road property. Except for those who are Caldwell kin, I find it rare to discover anyone in the modern day who has any knowledge of the Caldwell period of ownership.

At the time of the Franklin Road property's sale to W. H. Soper in January 1923, it was publicly reported that Soper would make a home at Oak Hill. However, there is no record that Soper and his wife, Adele Smith Soper, ever lived in the Oak Hill mansion. Instead, Soper began to subdivide the property and sell off lots.

Issues of the *Tennessean* in May 1924 contained ads for the sale of lots in the "Oak Hill Farm Subdivision," the lots "part of the historical Van Leer Kirkman Country Estate, fronting both sides of Battery Boulevard and [the south side of] Glendale Road."[1] At least 46 lots are shown on the ad's map.

It is not known why the Sopers did not move to the property. Evidently, they did not move to Nashville at all, for the deed transferring the 378 acres to Rogers Caldwell was executed in Monongalia County, West Virginia. The Sopers were gone, but their name remained forever in the first subdivision of the Oak Hill Farm. Soper Avenue today connects Battery Lane with Glendale Lane, just blocks away from First Presbyterian Church.

On December 15, 1925, Nashville businessman Rogers Caldwell bought the 378-acre Oak Hill Farm from the Sopers. The transaction

"W. H. Soper Sells Some of Kirkman Farm Land." Ad in *Nashville Tennessean*, May 25, 1924. Courtesy of Tennessee State Library and Archives.

included Caldwell taking over the promissory notes that Soper had executed when he purchased the property from Kate Kirkman in 1923. In addition, Caldwell promised to pay two years of taxes and took over several remodeling debts. Soper had created Oak Hill Subdivision in 1924 and began selling lots on 170 of the farm's acres, but the buyers did not own the property outright and started paying Caldwell instead of Soper. The deed for the Soper-to-Caldwell transaction is quite interesting, for it makes clear several notable neighbors whose lands were touched by the 378 acres. These included the Overton (Travellers Rest) property; the Thompson Glen Leven property; the Overton Lea property; and the Glendale Park property of James E. Caldwell. James E. Caldwell was Rogers' father.[2]

Family Background

For all that will be said here about Rogers Caldwell and his accomplishments, one must note that he was, first, the privileged son of a very wealthy Nashville family. James E. Caldwell, Rogers' father, was born in Memphis prior to the Civil War. The family moved after James was born, to Leflore County, Mississippi, to a 2,000-acre cotton farm on the Yazoo River, which was in James' mother's family. Her name was Sheppard, and the plantation was called Sheppardtown. Some fifty to sixty enslaved people were part of the estate.

The family moved several times after the war, eventually settling in Franklin, Tennessee, in 1867. James attended the University of Nashville, now Vanderbilt property, and worked in banking. He married May Winston. James became President of Fourth and First National Bank of Nashville and was also a leader in selling fire insurance. He was early into the telephone business in Nashville and became President of the Cumberland Telephone and Telegraph Co.; later, he sold the company to Southern Bell Telephone and Telegraph for $20,000,000, remaining with the business as Chairman of the Board. James was also President of the Union Stock Yards in Nashville, a thirty-five-year Trustee of Peabody College, and the president of a life insurance company in Missouri.

Photo from *The Peabody Reflector*, 41, no. 5, September-October 1968. Caldwell was a Trustee of the Peabody College for Teachers in Nashville. Courtesy of Tennessee State Library and Archives.

James built the streetcar line from downtown Nashville, which connected to the Glendale Park amusement park and zoo; he developed the rail line because he created the Glendale Park establishment. James also created a subdivision along the rail line, the Waverly Park neighborhood. To develop Glendale Park, the rail line, and the new neighborhood, he had to form a syndicate to buy extensive acreage in the area—all from Van Leer Kirkman, who owned much land south of Nashville.

The Caldwell home estate was called Longview, located on Franklin Road, where (now) Caldwell Lane intersects. The current Cofer Chapel Free Will Baptist Church is located on what was Longview property. Longview was a wasteland property after the Civil War; the Caldwells turned it into a beautiful 1500-acre estate. Family lore had it that there was nothing between Longview and the Kirkman estate except places to roam. The Longview mansion is now owned by Lipscomb University, as are the adjacent soccer fields.

The Caldwells were all members of First Presbyterian Church. One of Walter Courtenay's early funerals after his arrival in 1944 as the new pastor was the funeral in September 1944 of James E. Caldwell. It was conducted at the Longview home.

Rogers Caldwell's Rise to Wealth and Power

James E. and May Winston Caldwell had ten children, one of whom was named Rogers. We say again that Rogers was born into wealth and privilege. What more he did with his life would surprise even his parents. After dropping out of Vanderbilt University, he went into the fire insurance business with his father. It soon became apparent that Rogers had other skills. He was once described as "an insurance man who had drifted into bond buying because he had become interested in highway building through writing surety bonds for road contractors."³

Margaret Trousdale Caldwell

Margaret Trousdale Caldwell. Courtesy of Will and Cissy Caldwell Akers.

Rogers became so adept at what he did that he was a millionaire by age thirty. He created his own company, Caldwell and Company, in 1916, which soon had offices all over the South. A newspaperman in a southern city said, "In 10 years Rogers Caldwell will own everything."[4]

It did seem that way. In the 1920s, Caldwell began averaging $100 million in annual business; by about 1929, he had $650 million in assets. He created his own bank, the Bank of Tennessee, to handle most of his finances. The State of Tennessee itself was heavily invested in bonds controlled by Caldwell and Company.[5] Described as "the biggest wheel in the South," Caldwell and his empire were unimaginably huge. He controlled seventy-five banks; a half-dozen insurance companies; three newspapers; hotels; department stores; textile mills; mines; oil companies; a laundry; and the Nashville Vols baseball team.[6]

A thorough study of Rogers Caldwell is beyond the scope of this book; however, such information is readily available and is most interesting. Indeed, a major subchapter of a history of Nashville is devoted to Caldwell's part in the evolution of the banking and finance industry in Nashville.[7] How much personal faith was placed in Caldwell himself is reflected in an extraordinary newspaper quote from 1928:

> Rogers Caldwell is the Moses that will lead us out of … bondage and make possible for us a new freedom such as the old South has struggled for since the days of the Confederacy.[8]

Not everyone was on Caldwell's side as he rose in wealth and power. His detractors were sufficiently numerous and outspoken that someone thought it would help if his pastor put in a good word on his behalf. It shows the remarkable power that the pulpit of First Presbyterian Church was in those days that the *Tennessean* would put on page one a quote from Dr. James I. Vance defending Caldwell. In part, Vance said, "Rogers Caldwell is a citizen of the highest standing in personal character, business integrity, and service to the public."[9] Caldwell was a Deacon at First Presbyterian.

During his meteoric rise to fame and fortune, Caldwell purchased the Van Leer Kirkman Oak Hill estate. The 1925 purchase of the

378-acre property gave Rogers and Margaret Trousdale Caldwell a place to live and entertain while a new house of their own was being built nearby. The house, to be called Brentwood Hall, was to be erected on Franklin Road on Caldwell land, at the far eastern end of Hogan Road at Edmondson Pike.[10] But before Caldwell's dream house, Brentwood Hall (or Brentwood House), could be erected, a smaller house that Caldwell had built was moved off that property to a Franklin Road location at the intersection of Thompson Lane. Caldwell's friend and Vice-President of Caldwell and Company, Edward J. Heitzeberg, rented that house for many years.[11]

Oak Hill was a place of frequent social events when the Kirkmans were in residence. The tradition continued with the Caldwells. The society pages in the mid-1920s were full of news of the Caldwell doings:

> Mrs. Rogers Caldwell entertained delegates of a meeting of the Association of Junior Leagues of America, as her guests at Oak Hill.[12]

> The Ladies Battlefield Park Association met at Oak Hill, entertained by Mrs. Rogers Caldwell. Mrs. James E. Caldwell reported on efforts to get President Calvin Coolidge to attend the monument unveiling.[13]

A favorite saying of Rogers Caldwell hung in a frame at Oak Hill, then later at Brentwood Hall:

> While in this house, please do not say anything unkind about anyone, bearing in mind that what you think of others is nothing like as important as what others may think of you.[14]

The Crash of 1929 and the Fall of Caldwell's Empire

Caldwell was known as a quiet and kind man. However, it is sure that unkind things were thought about him when his empire tumbled as the stock market crashed in 1929 and the Great Depression settled upon the South. The Bank of Tennessee, a subdivision of Caldwell and Company, had so many State of Tennessee tax dollars and investments in it that the State, in effect, had become an affiliate of the company. When Caldwell and Company failed in September 1930, 120 banks in seven states, including the Bank of Tennessee, went down with it. It was a financial and political nightmare for Caldwell and his partner, Luke Lea. The nightmare was long and complicated. Luke Lea and his son Luke Jr. went to prison. Caldwell did not.

Though every bank in Tennessee seemed to go down with Caldwell and Company, it is of great historical interest, particularly to Nashvillians, that the Commerce Union Bank of Edward J. Potter did not fail. In his book about Potter's life and times, Jesse Hill Ford tells how Nashville's youngest bank President (Potter) almost got carried away with the excitement of Caldwell's rise to power but ultimately would not risk allying Commerce Union Bank with Caldwell. Furthermore, Potter, when asked, refused to help bail Caldwell out when the big crash came.[15] The State of Tennessee pursued Caldwell and his assets for decades afterward, finally taking over the Brentwood Hall mansion and property in a 1957 auction on the courthouse steps. That is why the state owns that property today, now known as the Ellington Agricultural Center. Some 207 acres were part of that seizure.[16]

Caldwell, who had become a First Presbyterian Church deacon in the 1920s at First Presbyterian Church when the church was still in downtown Nashville, continued his attendance there after the congregation moved to its Franklin Pike/Oak Hill location. Caldwell descendants today recall visiting Uncle Rogers at Brentwood Hall on weekends. He or Margaret would bring them to Sunday School on the Franklin Road campus. When the State took over Brentwood Hall, Rogers and Margaret moved to a small home in Franklin.

After the Caldwells moved into their mansion in 1928, which was patterned exactly like Andrew Jackson's "Hermitage," they sold the Kirkman Oak Hill Farm on July 31, 1929, to Frank L. Cheek. Cheek was one of the eleven children of Joel Owsley Cheek, founder of the Cheek-Neal Coffee Company.[17]

Chapter Five

The Cheek Family: 1929–1949

With the 1929 sale of the Franklin Road property to Frank L. Cheek, it might be said that the transition to the modern era began. There is no evidence that Rogers Caldwell made any substantive changes to the Kirkmans' Oak Hill home or estate when he and Margaret Caldwell occupied the property. We don't know what the Caldwells did with what may have been left of any livestock operations from the Kirkman era. One can only speculate about Frank Cheek's motivation for buying the large property. He may have witnessed the subdivision possibilities already initiated by W. H. Soper and desired to continue the process with the rest of the property.

Frank L. Cheek

Frank L. Cheek was the seventh son of Joel Owsley Cheek—there were eight sons and three daughters in all. Frank was married first to Elizabeth Hale, then to Marie Walters, by whom their daughter, Patricia, was born. At different (but sometimes overlapping) times, Frank had interesting businesses. He was President of the Board of Governors of the Food Products Institute of America.[1] He was also Managing Director of the advertising company in New York that advertised Maxwell House Coffee. Roast houses for the coffee were opened in Houston, Texas, and Brooklyn, New York. Some of this advertising involved a novel new medium—posters.[2]

Joel Owsley Cheek and his cousin, Christopher T. Cheek, both wholesale grocers, started a business in the 1890s known as the Nashville Coffee and Manufacturing Company. They had the idea that coffee beans could be blended, roasted, and packaged for retail sale, and they started a business based on that premise. Prior to this, people bought beans (called green beans), then took them home for roasting and grinding. In 1900, they partnered with J. W. Neal to form the Cheek-Neal Coffee Company. Owsley Cheek would be the first—and only—President.[3] The coffee operation was in a multi-story warehouse at 148 2nd Avenue in downtown Nashville.[4] At some point, the coffee entrepreneurs persuaded the prestigious Maxwell House Hotel at 4th Avenue and Church Street to serve Cheek-Neal's blended coffee exclusively in its restaurants. In a genius move, the Cheeks and Neal offered to call the coffee Maxwell House Coffee. This advertising move proved to be a winning idea; the growth in popularity of the coffee and the accompanying profitability of the business was astounding. In 1928, the Cheek-Neal Coffee Company was sold to the Postum Company for over $40 million. Postum became Maxwell House Products Company, then General Foods, followed by Kraft Foods, and today the company is Kraft Heinz.

Frank L. Cheek was a Vice-President of Cheek-Neal, so it follows that he shared in the great windfall of money which came to the Cheeks. His share of profits gave him the means to purchase the Oak Hill property from Rogers Caldwell.

Nearby, a sister of Frank L. Cheek, Helen Ritchey Cheek Farrell, the wife of Herbert Farrell, moved onto another Overton property. The Farrells bought the Overton Hall estate and renamed it Crieve Hall. This property was in the Stillwood Drive, Crieve Road/ Hogan Road area.

Little can be found in newspapers or public records about Frank L. Cheek's tenure as owner of Oak Hill. However, one interesting—and puzzling—item was in a 1930 newspaper social column. The column writer said, "Wonder why the Frank Cheeks have stopped work on the construction of their new home now that the demolition of the old mansion at 'Oak Hill' has been completed?"[5]

Connecting the Dots

Since many newcomers to the First Presbyterian Franklin Road property already have a hazy notion of a connection between the church's Cheek House and Maxwell House Coffee, it may be helpful at this point to connect a few dots to show the real picture. It's a little complicated:

- Col. John Overton decided that Nashville needed a quality hotel and that he would be the one to build it. He began a grand hotel at the corner of 4th Avenue and Church Street (then called Cherry Street and Spring Street) in 1859. The Civil War intervened, and the unfinished structure was used for Union Army purposes during that time.

- The hotel was finished in 1869; Overton named it the Maxwell House Hotel. The name honored his wife, Harriet Virginia Maxwell Overton.

- Harriet Virginia Maxwell was a daughter of Jesse Maxwell Jr. [1796–1856] and Martha A. Claiborne [1809–1845 or 1847]. Harriet's grandfather, Jesse Maxwell Sr., was the very person who secured the 640-acre North Carolina Land Grant #367 for the heirs of David Maxwell. Jesse Sr. also secured a 640-acre grant for himself next to his brother David's grant. The David Maxwell grant became the basis for Judge John Overton's Travellers Rest, and the First Presbyterian Church property became part of its acreage.

- So, in this interesting way, the First Presbyterian Church property on Franklin Road has a connection to the original Maxwell owners of the North Carolina land grants.

The Sale of Oak Hill Farm to John Hancock Cheek

In October of 1933, Frank L. and Marie W. Cheek executed a Quitclaim Deed, selling for one dollar 187 acres of the Oak Hill Farm to his brother, John Hancock Cheek. The boundaries included Battery Road, Lealand Lane, Franklin Pike, and Overton Lea's line. The deed states that it was part of the same land conveyed to Caldwell and Company on November 16, 1926, and Frank L. Cheek on July 31, 1929.[6] The

John Hancock Cheek. Courtesy of Mrs. William Eason Jr. (Nancy).

same restrictive racial and structural covenants still existed and ran with the land.

John Hancock Cheek was the sixth of eight brothers who were sons of Joel Owsley Cheek, President of the Cheek-Neal Coffee Company. John H. Cheek was in the retail automobile business and owned Cumberland Motor Company, Inc. This company was the world's first

Dodge dealership. As such, Cheek rated a mention in Dodge's official history book:

> Dodge's first dealer was John H. Cheek of Nashville, Tennessee, son of Joel Cheek who founded Maxwell House Coffee. Joel urged John to go to Detroit to talk to the Dodge brothers. The first car sold on December 22, 1914. John Cheek sold WWI hero Sgt. Alvin York his first car, and also taught him to drive.[7]

John Cheek had previously worked with his father in the Cheek-Neal business and the Farrell-Cheek Steel Co., Sandusky, Ohio. His wife was Susan Anderson Glenn of Clarksville, Tennessee. In 1927 they purchased and moved into Braeburn, the home at 211 Deer Park Drive in the Belle Meade area of Nashville. In 1934, they and their three children, Susan, Eleanor Ritchie, and John H. Cheek Jr., moved into a new home they had built, choosing to keep the Kirkman home's name of Oak Hill for their home. Braeburn became the official Executive Residence of Vanderbilt University; most Chancellors have lived there.[8] Though it has been stated in published works that the Cheek's Oak Hill was built in 1930, it definitely was not. The First Presbyterian Archives preserve the 1934 architect plans; in addition, the current Cheek House has on the wall in the little library the 1934 landscaping plan for Oak Hill, rendered in December 1934.

Continuing the tradition of hosting Nashville's social elite on the property, the Cheek version of Oak Hill remained a well-known spot for parties and receptions, an early one being a meeting of the Peabody Aid Society.[9] The house was remarkable for its time, boasting air conditioning, handmade bricks, and a staircase made of ten thousand pieces of wood; front and back views of the house each looked like a front. Ten fireplaces and an intricate steam heat system helped warm the house.

The era of the John and Susan Cheek version of Oak Hill only lasted for about fifteen years, from 1934 until 1949, when First Presbyterian Church (FPC) bought the house and property from the Cheeks, who were members of the church. It is common for current members and visitors to FPC to place the building much farther back in history, even to the Civil War. This misunderstanding is one of several reasons this

Susan Glenn Cheek, 1916 wedding photo. Courtesy of Mrs. William Eason Jr. (Nancy).

book was written: to get a more accurate and realistic picture of the whole history of the property. Whatever the Cheeks may have thought in 1934, by 1949, it seemed to be the case that no one of the three children desired to own the property, and neither did John and Susan Cheek. It is known that John Cheek was not in good health at that time.

The Sunday bulletin at First Presbyterian Church on April 24, 1949, contained a call for a congregational meeting to be held on May 1 for the purpose of deciding whether to buy the Franklin Road property of church members John and Susan Cheek. The bulletin stated

Foyer of the Cheek home during the Cheek occupancy. Courtesy of Mrs. William Eason Jr. (Nancy).

that the house was designed by Warfield and Keeble and was built in 1934.[10] The same information was conveyed in a church newsletter.[11] The decision made on May 1, 1949, had a long prelude with great ramifications for the future of First Presbyterian Church of Nashville.

RECEPTION AT OAK HILL FOLLOWS EASON - CHEEK WEDDING SATURDAY—Following the marriage of Miss Susan Cheek to William Eason at Westminster Presbyterian Church Saturday evening, Mr. and Mrs. John Cheek, the bride's parents, entertained at a reception at Oak Hill, their home on Franklin Road. Pictured above are the bride's attendants. Reading from left to right, they are: Front row, Miss Margaret White, Mrs. William M. Wilson, matron of honor, Miss Eleanor Ritchey Cheek, sister of the bride who was the maid of honor;; Miss Elizabeth Howell and, Miss Elizabeth Rudolph of Springfield; ascending the stairs, Miss Virginia McClellan, Miss Damaris Witherspoon, Miss Camille Stone, Miss Shirley Caldwell, and Miss Florence Cheek, a cousin of the bride. Mr. and Mrs. Eason are pictured below, cutting th——

Wedding photo (1941) of William H. Eason Sr. and Susan Anderson Cheek, daughter of John and Susan Cheek. Staircase photo is the Cheek home, now First Presbyterian's "Cheek House." Fourth bridesmaid from the top on the staircase is Damaris Witherspoon, who many years later would write a three-volume history of First Presbyterian Church. Courtesy of Mrs. William Eason Jr. (Nancy).

Cheek recreation room during Cheek occupancy. The Cheek recreation room, with billiard table, became Stanford Chapel of First Presbyterian Church. Courtesy of Mrs. William Eason Jr. (Nancy).

Overhead beams were left when the Cheek recreation room was transformed into Stanford Chapel in 1953. The church referred to it as "Oak Hill Chapel" in the weekly bulletin until the 1955 removal to Franklin Road. Photo courtesy of First Presbyterian Church of Nashville Archives.

OAK HILL CHAPEL AND CHURCH HOUSE
FRANKLIN AND TYNE — NASHVILLE, TENNESSEE

Image on a brochure showing the rear view of the Oak Hill Chapel and Church House in 1949. Courtesy of First Presbyterian Church of Nashville Archives.

Cheek House of First Presbyterian Church with Stanford Chapel on the left. Photo taken in 2022. Courtesy of the author.

THE FIRST PRESBYTERIAN CHURCH
NASHVILLE, TENNESSEE
Photograph by John Hageman

Chapter Six

First Presbyterian Church of Nashville: 1949 to Present

This chapter in the story of the First Presbyterian Church property coincides with the church's own history. Throughout the chapter, there is a heavy reliance on the best and most comprehensive published history, Damaris Witherspoon Steele's *First Church: A History of Nashville First Presbyterian Church, Vols. 1, 2, 3.* If there is a particular need to be more specific within that framework, I have provided the citation in the endnotes. Other sources are, of course, also properly noted.

The Journey Toward Buying the Property

On May 1, 1949, a meeting of the congregation of First Presbyterian Church was held, the purpose being to vote on buying the John and Susan Cheek property, which was south of Nashville on Franklin Road at Tyne Boulevard. The proposal was approved, and the church officers quickly executed the agreement to purchase the Cheeks' home and approximately fifty-five acres of surrounding land for $116,000. The church had the option to buy the other 165 acres of the property but did not exercise that option. With this purchase, First Presbyterian Church acquired virtually the same rectangular piece of land Van Leer Kirkman bought from Col. John Overton in 1887. The difference between Kirkman's sixty-four-plus acres and the Cheek's fifty-five acres

---

Opposite page: Winter picture of Sanctuary, 1960s. Photo by John Hageman. Courtesy of First Presbyterian Church of Nashville Archives.

is accounted for by two lots along the north side of Tyne Boulevard, going in a westward direction. These adjacent lots constitute about nine acres. The lot most adjacent to the main Cheek property, at 850 Tyne Boulevard, had become the property of Susan Anderson Cheek and her new husband, William Howard Eason, when they married in 1941. It was purchased by First Presbyterian Church in 2010. Current First Presbyterian Church Clerk of Session John Cheek Eason grew up in that house, as did his older brothers William H. Eason Jr. and Glenn Wilder Eason. Bill Eason died during the preparation of this book. The house was eventually demolished. The next lot westward, 856 Tyne Boulevard, does not belong to the church; however, current members Duncan McKay Fort III, Sue Fort White, and Missy Fort Goodman knew that house as home while growing up, as did several generations of the DeWitt Thompson family, also First Presbyterian members.

Tensions in the 1940s—Catalysts for Change

The 1949 purchase of the Cheek property may seem abrupt on the face of it. It was not. From the church's perspective, the story behind the acquisition of this land was anything but abrupt. The decade of 1940 saw a succession of events that led to the purchase. These events were not always happy; they involved much controversy. It might be said that an entire decade and a half of tensions of one kind or another began in 1936 with the resignation of longtime pastor Dr. James I. Vance, who served from 1895–1900 and 1910–1936.

Pastor Vance's health forced him to retire in 1936. A committee to search for a new pastor was quickly assembled. Negative feelings arose during that committee's election because the committee formed was already disposed to call Assistant Pastor Thomas Calhoun Barr as the new pastor. Barr had been serving as Assistant Pastor since 1929. He was not altogether popular with the congregation, not being as good a preacher as Vance. Some people just did not favor him. However, without a proper search—the kind that a large congregation normally did—Barr was elected by the congregation only a month after Vance's resignation. Scores of people voted against Barr, including quite a few of the officers.

Actions by Thomas Barr not long after his installation further alienated sections of the congregation. A month into his tenure, he had the worn American flag removed from the Sanctuary. The removal was not permanent, but the new flag was only allowed to be displayed on certain occasions instead of regularly. The church's history notes that people did not forget this action, particularly as national tensions were rising as the country observed the great possibility of a war in Europe. Barr's popularity was further eroded as church attendance fell after his installation. A few members began sending their children to more suburban churches in areas where they resided, notably Moore Memorial Church and its outpost, Westminster Presbyterian. Even the Session and Diaconate were struggling to achieve as much as 50 percent attendance at their meetings.

By the time of the Pearl Harbor attack and shortly thereafter, First Presbyterian was fully invested in mobilizing for the war effort. Red Cross meetings were held at the church, bandages were rolled, and a Serviceman's Lounge was created. In addition, members were urged to take itinerant service members to lunch after church. The presbytery's committee for war work, a local part of the General Assembly's Defense Services Council, headquartered itself at First Presbyterian. At about this time, Thomas Barr, in a sermon, expressed the opinion "that the United States could have stayed out of the war, and now was the time to organize for the restoration of peace." A great exception was taken to this opinion by many in the congregation. Many older members had fought in World War I, and their patriotism was high; they also had sons in uniform, and pacifist sermons were not welcome.

Gathering unrest in the congregation led the Session in July 1942 to debate whether to instruct Barr to avoid certain topics in the pulpit; many supported that thought, but the majority supported Barr's right to choose. Later in July, at a joint meeting of officers, it was reported that nearly 700 church members had signed a petition stating that "conditions existed, which if continued, would be detrimental to our church and the work of the Lord Jesus Christ." The petition called for an immediate congregational meeting to express confidence in Thomas Calhoun Barr. Unfortunately, Barr and his family were on vacation during all this activity.

A committee was put together to draft a motion for the congregational meeting; however, the motion was broadened in a profoundly important way. Questions were to be answered in a yes/no fashion. This forced members not only to indicate a vote of confidence in their pastor but also to register an opinion on whether he could unify the congregation and whether his remaining pastor would promote the welfare of the church. At a meeting of the joint board of officers, the officers themselves answered the questions. Remarkably, a huge majority of the officers voted that a pastoral change would be best. A congregational meeting was never held. Things got so tricky for the Session that the presbytery's Commission on the Minister and His Work was called in to sort out the difficulties at First Presbyterian Church of Nashville. After multiple meetings with all the groups at odds with each other, the commission declared that the best thing for the church would be for Thomas C. Barr to leave. The commission dissolved the pastoral relationship between Barr and the church, effective September 14, 1942. Two hundred and sixteen members of First Presbyterian Church left the church over this issue (only one Elder), choosing to start a new congregation nearby and to persuade Thomas Barr to be the founding pastor. Thus, Trinity Presbyterian Church was organized on December 15, 1942.

In November 1942, Dr. Oliver C. Carmichael, Chancellor of Vanderbilt University and an elder at First Church, was appointed chairman of a committee to search for a new pastor. Eleven months later, on October 31, 1943, the committee recommended to the congregation Walter Rowe Courtenay, a Princeton Seminary classmate of Westminster Presbyterian's William Phifer, who was to arrive in early 1944. Courtenay was installed on February 13, 1944.

Walter Courtenay was a strong leader, not afraid to wade into situations that, in his view, needed changing. He recognized that he had moved to a congregation that had suffered a recent and painful division. Further, he realized that his new church was in a location that did not favor growth and youth work and that the idea of relocation was already a topic.[1]

A Need for Change and the Building Survey Committee

On October 6, 1944, the joint board of elders and deacons heard a report of a committee appointed in either late 1943 or early 1944 to look into making changes to the inadequate Sunday School building. During the investigation, the Building Survey Committee had hired an expert consultant, a Dr. Conover, from the International Bureau of Architects in New York City. They were specialists in Sunday School buildings. It was Conover's opinion that $150,000 would improve the structure, but it would still be inadequate. He thought that $200,000–$250,000 would put the church and Sunday School building in good shape, including the addition of air conditioning. However, his clear recommendation to the committee was to sell the whole property and relocate to a Vanderbilt-area location. He believed the downtown property could be sold for $500,000, enough to relocate and build anew.

Each recommendation was controversial in its own way, a lot of money being at stake in each case. Walter Courtenay was not publicly favoring any particular course of action but did report to the church officers the current demographics of the church membership. It was clear that nearly all the new families were coming from suburban locations. He also noted that, in general, urban churches tend to evolve into communities of older and single people, not youth and families. The joint board decided that the Conover suggestion of relocation should be investigated before any decision was made on renovations.

The joint board also decided that the congregation should know what was afoot, so a congregational meeting was held on Tuesday, October 24. Everything the congregation heard at that meeting was put into a slick-paper booklet and mailed to each household.[2] The Reports document bears the heavy imprint of Jesse Wills, who chaired the Building Survey Committee (technically, he chaired for the Session; Clark Hutton was listed as Chairman for the Deacons). Wills provided an extensive commentary on all aspects of the Building Survey Committee and its reports. At that time, he was Chairman of the

National Life and Accident Insurance Company, founded by his father, William Ridley Wills. In 1925 the company created the WSM radio station as a marketing tool, which gave rise to the Grand Ole Opry radio show, a tool for further marketing. Jesse Wills was quite a capable writer, having been a part of the famous Fugitives poetry and literature group centered at Vanderbilt University. He began with that group as an undergraduate student in the 1920s.

Shortly after this Building Survey Committee report was out, Walter Courtenay's November 12, 1944, sermon, "The Future of Old First," spoke of changes underway at First Presbyterian Church, with strong hints of more to come. No one could miss the theme of change. By this time, Courtenay had already changed up the worship service, instituted a rotation system of officers, consolidated all women's groups into one Women of the Church organization, and hired a new organist and a choir director. The possibility of relocation was not avoided; however, it should be noted that Elder Jesse Wills took every opportunity to absolve Courtenay of the instigation of this subject. The Building Survey Committee was not Courtenay's committee, and he did not hire the consultant, Conover. In fact, it is not outside the realm of possibility that Conover, a close friend of former pastor James I. Vance, floated the subject with Vance in the 1930s. Conover was known to have visited the church during Vance's time as pastor.

Late in 1947, the Building Survey Committee was heard from again, with majority and minority reports regarding what to do next. It wanted to survey the congregation about three options: (1) stay and do nothing, (2) stay and renovate, or (3) relocate. Walter Courtenay slowed the Committee down by pointing out that the Christmas season was not the time for controversial subjects; early 1948 would be soon enough. By this time, another factor had arisen, complicating all discussion: The two daily newspapers in Nashville, the *Banner* and the *Tennessean*, had gotten wind of the conversations about relocation and had written articles and editorials on the subject.

The Session, in January 1948, did authorize a survey of the congregation. At the same time, the deacons voted a resolution to the Session, urging them to call a congregational meeting as soon as the survey results were received. The Diaconate membership was heavily weighted toward the younger men of the congregation, whose families represented the same kinds of families living in the suburbs which were defecting to other churches or not attracted to a church like First Presbyterian in the first place.

By the June Session meeting, only 152 surveys had been returned, this from a membership of 1,500. The survey results were as follows:

- 10—Stay downtown and do nothing.
- 40—Relocate the congregation.
- 83—Stay downtown, make improvements, and extend the ministry.
- 19—No vote was indicated, but written remarks were made.

The analysis committee noted a strong push toward "establishing a suburban mission, youth center, or chapel in another part of town."[3]

The Decision to Renovate and Expand Services

At the April 1948 joint board meeting, a committee was authorized to create a plan for renovating downtown facilities and searching for a suburban location for selected activities previously discussed. So, at last, official eyes were now looking at potential suburban properties, in the Vanderbilt area, out Hillsboro Road, and on Franklin Road.

Walter Courtenay had often stated that he could live with the church remaining downtown if that was the congregation's preference. But there can be no doubt that he would be happier with a new location. He recalls that respected Elder R. D. Stanford took him to lunch one day and pushed for the idea of relocation "for the good of the congregation." Courtenay said, "since he was a real estate executive, I took his opinion seriously."[4] In the same recollection, he remembers that Jesse Wills was very much in favor of finding suburban property for youth and family ministry.

Courtenay described the sudden appearance of just such a property in this way:

> In 1948, I learned that the 200-acre John Cheek property might be for sale. [He already knew the property well, the Cheeks being members, and Courtenay having had meetings and youth fellowships there]. I learned this on a Sunday morning. On Monday morning, I was talking to Susan Cheek in the recreation room [of the Cheek's home]. I asked her if the Cheeks would be willing to sell 55 acres and all the buildings to her church. With tears in her eyes, she said that it would be an answer to her prayers.

By April 1949, an option for First Presbyterian Church to buy the Cheek home and property was prepared. The thirty-day option gave time for officers and members to visit the property prior to a decision. The property was pitched as a place for a weekday preschool, a suburban Sunday School, youth meetings, a day camp, and a chapel for weddings and funerals. The purchase price would be $116,000 for the house and about fifty acres, with an option to buy 165 additional acres. On May 1, First Presbyterian Church bought fifty-five acres and the buildings for the agreed $116,000. It chose not to buy the other acreage, which lay behind and northward of the property.

Newspaper coverage of the May 1 congregational vote reported the tally as 486 for and 39 against the plan. It noted that there were some "sharp verbal exchanges." Church plans not previously published were brought forth: All Sunday night youth meetings would be at the Oak Hill location, and preaching services on Wednesdays and Sundays were planned.[5] One must wonder if those opposed to this plan for suburban outreach and ministry were thinking further into the future. Not only was the vigor represented by families and youth about to leave the downtown scene, but the new possibility of preaching at Oak Hill could easily be imagined as a prelude to the total relocation of the church. They now had the property to carry it off.

Though the church did not buy the extra 165 acres, it is apparent from copies of correspondence in the church archives that it got a kind of bonus from the unpurchased property. The committee from the church which negotiated the Cheek sale made an exclusive arrangement with the Dobson-Bainbridge Realty Company to profit from the future sale of the 165 acres not bought. With the approval of the Cheeks, the church was to receive the profit, less commission, if the 165 acres of the option sold for more than the option price.[6]

Using the New Property

The church wasted no time after the Cheek property was purchased. Immediately, a sixteen-page booklet (untitled) was published, describing the house and property and the church's plans for the future. "Oak Hill is ours!" one section began. "We say it with pride and gratitude. To our downtown church, we have added this suburban place of loveliness. Now we can have the advantages of two locations and thus do a greater and more permanent work for God and the Kingdom."[7]

The same booklet outlined the ambitious plans already in place for Fall 1949. At publication, thirty-four children from three and a half to five years of age were enrolled in a five-day nursery and kindergarten. The school would operate from 9:00 a.m. until 3:00 p.m.; the annual cost for each child was $210, including the lunch meal!

A committee to build a new manse at the new location was also organized. The Courtenays had been living since 1944 in a home on Lauderdale Avenue near Vanderbilt.

As might have been predicted, the church soon found itself trying to decide between a rapid expansion of the new Oak Hill holdings and renovation and repair of the downtown property. Just as the church was purchasing the Oak Hill property, a 1949 report from Hart, Freeland, and Roberts architects appeared, summarizing what would be needed in the way of necessary improvements to the two downtown buildings, the Sanctuary and Sunday School buildings. This company had undertaken improvements in 1938 to the twin towers and roof of the main building. The cost for the recommended work in 1949 was over $247,000, quite a shock to the congregation. The report floated around for several years. Not only would the work be expensive, but it would also be controversial, for the architectural firm had followed through with the suggestion from one faction of the congregation that some of the Egyptian aspects be modified. The proposal called for removing all Egyptian motifs from the interior and exterior of the buildings. This idea had to have come from Walter Courtenay, who, from the beginning of his pastorate in 1944, was not enamored with the Egyptian flavor of the property. Many in the congregation did not share his opinion since they had grown up in the 1850s building.[8]

At the Oak Hill property, worship began early after the acquisition, using the Cheek recreation room (a billiard room). The billiard table had quickly gone to the attic. Attendance soon outgrew the small space of the recreation room. People expressed the wish to build a separate chapel on the Oak Hill property. A different plan eventually came about, which saw the former billiard room transformed into a cross-shaped chapel. The primary impetus for the project was a gift from Robert, Harold, and Myrtle Stanford, in memory of their father, longtime First Presbyterian Elder Robert D. Stanford, who had died in 1944. Other significant gifts came from in memory of Mrs. Kendrick C. Hardcastle, Mrs. Felix Bard, William Anderson Spickard, Mrs. R. L. Proctor, and Mrs. Edwin Price.[9] The Stanford Chapel was built and was already in constant use when it was dedicated on September 13, 1953.

Relocating the Congregation

At the February 1954 Session meeting, a petition came forth, signed by forty-two church members:

> We, the undersigned members of First Presbyterian Church, Nashville, do Petition and request that the Session authorize a complete, long-range Survey of the Oak Hill properties, in order to plan for an adequate Church and educational plant at Oak Hill. This is necessary at the earliest Possible time due to the increasing problems arising as our church grows.[10]

Minutes of that meeting show that the moderator, Dr. Courtenay, was authorized to appoint a committee to propose "what should be done."

Damaris Steele, the church historian, offered the opinion that "an argument can be made that the official beginning of the plan to relocate First Presbyterian Church dates from this meeting."[11]

Staring the newly formed committee in the face was a denominational end-of-1953 statistical report which showed that the 1,756 members of First Presbyterian Church of Nashville now owned Oak Hill properties (new manse included) valued at $1,200,000 and the Church Avenue/5th Avenue property valued at $750,000. Spending was being called for at both locations. Sunday School growth at Oak Hill was increasing at a staggering rate. Classes were meeting not only in the buildings on campus but also in the Robertson Academy gymnasium next door. Further, children's classes were being held on the church property in old, converted buses, which an enterprising church officer had arranged to be brought to the campus and fixed up for classrooms. Meanwhile, the giant $247,635 proposal for the downtown property was still awaiting a decision.

A Church Divided

Dr. Courtenay's family returned in September 1954 from a late-summer vacation to a congregation divided within itself. The downtown Sunday School was shrinking, and it had become obvious that families attending activities at Oak Hill were not interested in going downtown to any church functions. Further, the new nursery school and kindergarten were wildly successful, with waiting lists for both. Everyone began to understand that the church's money for the future was now in the pockets of its suburban members.

On October 20, 1954, the Session voted thirteen to five (with three abstentions) to call a congregational meeting for Wednesday, November 10, 7:30 p.m., to hear a report of both the planning committee and the finance committee, and

> ... if the way be clear, to authorize the officers of the church, in the discretion of the Session, to relocate the First Presbyterian Church to the Oak Hill site at Franklin Road and Tyne Blvd., to lease or sell the downtown site at 5th Ave. and Church Street, and to

use the proceeds of such lease or sale to help defer the cost of relocating the First Presbyterian Church. A copy of the resolution shall be printed and distributed to the congregation with the church bulletin dated Sunday October 24, 1954, or October 31, 1954.[12]

The resolution was distributed on October 31 with an additional proviso that the Session would not exercise its discretionary authority unless a substantial majority, not less than 60% of those voting, voted in favor. The November 10 congregational meeting was held as scheduled. Those favoring relocation numbered 673; those against were 327. Exactly 1,000 members voted that night.

The church's three-volume narrative history tells much more about the internal debates leading up to this vote. The bulletins and newsletters of the church were "terse and sparse," but newspaper accounts were neither. The papers loved the "fight" and delighted in writing about "the Fighting First." Following the vote, the newspapers tended to favor the losing side, portraying those who wanted to leave downtown as villains.[13]

It probably surprised many people in Nashville the day after the vote to see an architect's drawing in the *Tennessean* (November 11, 1954) of the complete, new, proposed physical plant on Franklin Road, with Sanctuary, Cheek House, Educational Building, and a colonnade connecting all the buildings. These plans had not been revealed before this. In fact, Warfield and Associates architects had created drawings as early as September 29 (plans are in the church's archives).

While the Session and other church leaders worked on plans to sell or lease the downtown property and physically relocate First Presbyterian Church, the minority, who voted against relocation, mobilized. They initiated a complaint to the Nashville Presbytery (area governing body of Presbyterians), claiming that the voting procedure on November 10 was flawed and that Walter Courtenay had unduly influenced the process. The complaint was presented to a meeting of the presbytery at Glen Leven Presbyterian Church on January 18, 1955. The presbytery then referred the complaint to its Judicial Committee, which submitted its report to a January 25 meeting of the presbytery.

After reviewing that report, the presbytery sustained the Session's handling of the November vote, clearing the way for the move.

Though there were threats of appeal to higher denominational governing bodies, the Session proceeded to seek bids for the sale of the downtown property. Several offers were discussed at the March 1955 deacons' meeting and the April Session meeting. Several offers had come to the church, one for $750,000 for the downtown land and buildings. By the time of the April Session meeting, the minority group had organized itself well enough that it sent its own purchase proposal to be considered. It offered $350,000, hoping that it could organize a new church in the old buildings. The Session declined this offer but countered with an offer to sell for $550,000. The committee formed to do these negotiations for the minority did not have this kind of money; however, a plan was pieced together with the help of a bank loan and a gift of $100,000 from esteemed church leader Jesse Wills. The entire amount of $550,000 was to be paid to First Presbyterian Church by October 1, 1955.

Moving Pains and Decisions

Relocating the church to the suburban location involved decisions about everything, large and small, in the downtown buildings, from inconsequential supplies to heavy furnishings, church files, archival files, and historical items. The list takes up many pages in Session records of the time. A prior agreement about certain fairly permanent items physically attached to the buildings led to quite a bit of bitterness when the final agreement was signed. That prior agreement, accomplished by a small committee, did not appear in the final agreement. These items included the huge outside tablature pieces on the Church Street side of the building and three very large, heavy plaques that honored three past well-known pastors. The smooth stone plaques were permanently attached to the wall of the Narthex. Before anyone knew quite what happened, the historical record of the church's history and its roll of pastors was painted over with black paint, and the three plaques were ripped off the wall, causing much damage to the wall and one of the plaques. A dated cornerstone was also clumsily chiseled out of an outside wall of the Sunday School building. The minority group was very unhappy, and the newspapers happily took the side of those members trying to preserve the buildings. Sadly, the items coming from downtown overwhelmed the ability of the church to find a place to store them at the Oak Hill location. It is highly likely that historical items were just lost in the process. The Narthex plaques honoring James I. Vance, John Todd Edgar, and Thomas V. Moore ended up in the Cheek House basement, where they reside to this day.

On May 29, 1955, a congregational meeting was held after the 11:00 a.m. worship service. The congregation confirmed the sale of the downtown property, and five new trustees were elected: T. H. Mitchell, C. H. Hutton, William J. Wade, Henry Boyd, and Louis J. Allen. That was the last Sunday service of First Presbyterian Church at the Church and 5th location.

Sunday, June 5, 1955, was the official first day that all of First Presbyterian Church's operations were located at the Oak Hill property on Franklin Road (technically, June 1 was the day of "vacating" the downtown property). The June 5 worship bulletin no longer had the sketch of the twin-towered downtown buildings, but it had the architect's rendering of the proposed Sanctuary, connected by a covered colonnade to the Cheek home. The street address "4815 Franklin Road" first appeared in that June 5 bulletin. The Cheek residence, by this time, had become known by most as "the church house." The proposed first educational building, prominently next to the Sanctuary in the sketch published in the newspaper the day after the 1954 vote to move, was not on the bulletin. Church officers had revised the site plan, deciding to locate the educational building to the rear of the proposed Sanctuary.

The June 5 worship service was followed by an outside congregational dinner. People scattered to tables and stone walls in the rear of the Church House, around old buses that had been placed around the campus, and in the parking area near Cannon Youth Center. The buses had been obtained as temporary Sunday School classes for children and were a unique feature of the Oak Hill campus. When the move from downtown was made, two of them became offices for secretarial staff members.

Following the congregational dinner, the hundreds of people in attendance moved to a portion of the property that had been prepared as a groundbreaking site by the architects and builders. The groundbreaking ceremony was for both the Sanctuary and the Educational Building. The Session had decided that the Educational Building would actually be built first and quickly, the need being so great. This building was designed to be used by the nursery school, the kindergarten, and the Sunday School. There is no doubt that each building was urgently needed. Sunday worship services became even more jam-packed with the move, with folding chairs down the hall to other parts of the Church House and even outside. Closed-circuit viewing was provided for people in other rooms in the Church House.

The groundbreaking day was sunny and warm. Music director Cyrus Daniel led the gathered crowd in singing "Onward Christian Soldiers." Several men spoke, including Allen Dobson, the Chairman of the Building Committee. Mrs. Charles Sykes, the oldest active member of the congregation at the time, was on hand and sitting in a special chair. Walter Courtenay, using a special shovel, which is still in the church archives, turned over some dirt. And representing the great need for educational space was a young girl, Ida Hamilton Thompson Gayden, described in the ceremony's printed program as the great-great-great granddaughter of Judge John Overton; he had bought the property in 1796 and 1800 from William and Moses Maxwell. Little Ida was also identified as the great-great-great-great granddaughter of Ann Grundy (Mrs. Felix), a member of the church in its 1814 official organizing year, and the founder of the first Sunday School in Nashville in 1820. A large painted portrait of Mrs. Grundy still hangs in the Cheek House. The groundbreaking service ended with the singing of "Blest Be the Tie That Binds."

Everything from the downtown buildings was immediately jammed into the Cheek home or two of the old Sunday School buses, which were turned into secretarial offices. This "everything" meant office equipment and supplies, classroom furniture, historical files, memorabilia—whatever one might imagine would need to go if one were to move from one place to another. It is likely true that any number of things had to

Groundbreaking for the new Sanctuary and the new education building, June 5, 1955. Pictured are Dr. Walter R. Courtenay and Mrs. Charles E. Sykes (Ella Gillespie Sykes). Courtesy of First Presbyterian Church of Nashville.

Ida Hamilton Thompson Gayden at the 1955 groundbreaking. Courtesy of First Presbyterian Church of Nashville.

go to people's homes just to have someplace to go. We will never know what items were eventually lost to history in this rapid move.

The Education Building was completed in short order, and the dedication and occupation of this highly anticipated structure took place on December 23, 1956, the very same day that the cornerstone for the Sanctuary was dedicated. The 1956 cornerstone is still very visible from the front porch of the Sanctuary.

The Sanctuary itself was dedicated on November 24, 1957, in a memorable worship service that featured the Moderators of the Session, the Presbytery of Nashville, the Synod of Tennessee, and even William M. Elliott, Jr., Moderator of the General Assembly of the Presbyterian Church in the United States. Elliott was the pastor of Highland Park Presbyterian Church in Dallas, Texas. That same afternoon, Cyrus Daniel played concert pieces on the new carillon bells, and a short service was presided over by Dr. Walter Courtenay. On Monday night, November 25, the new Casavant Freres pipe organ was dedicated with a recital by Cyrus Daniel. Capping the week was a Thanksgiving Day service on Thursday featuring the Sanctuary Choir. "Psalm 68—A Festival Cantata" composed by Cyrus Daniel, was premiered during that service.

Major Buildings and Projects: 1934–2022

This book does not propose to relive the whole history of First Presbyterian's time on Franklin Road. However, it might be helpful to list major buildings and projects for historical purposes so that there is a (more or less) chronological record of those buildings and projects. (Oak Hill School does not fit precisely into these categories, but it was a major thrust of ministry.)

- Cheek House and Cheek garage—both built in 1934; five-car garage became Cannon Youth Center.
- 1949—weekday kindergarten began.
- Cannon Youth Center—1951—renovation of the Cheek five-car garage creates a home for junior high, senior high, and college Sunday night fellowships. Named for Lt. Edward C. Cannon, son-in-law of Elder and Mrs. Allen Dobson, who funded and

oversaw the project. Cannon was killed in action in 1944. After the church's 1955 move, the building became the home of the church's Boy Scout Troop 217.

- Tyne House—Manse for pastors; Walter Courtenay the first to occupy, in January, 1952.
- Stanford Chapel created from recreation room—1953; worship services held there for several years before the renovation was done.
- Educational building—dedicated Sunday, December 23, 1956; now called C Wing.
- Sanctuary—cornerstone laid, 1956; occupied, November 24, 1957; Architects: Warfield and Associates; Builders: J. A. Jones, Co., Charlotte, North Carolina.
- Elementary school proposed—1957; did not result in a school at First Presbyterian, but Ensworth School came out of the initiative
- Sullivan Garden—memorial to Jennie and Bob Sullivan and Miss Amanda Coke, Jennie's sister. The garden area, with brick crosswalks, was created between Sanctuary and Cheek House with the erection of the Sanctuary. Was likely not named until the 1960s deaths of the Sullivans and Miss Coke. In later years, the upper part of the garden area was fashioned into a "Biblical Garden" by Gladys Hamilton (Mrs. Charles H.). The ashes of the Hamiltons were scattered in that area, near where there is a fountain today; plaques on the brick wall there memorialize the Hamiltons.
- Church House/Cheek home officially designated by Session as "Cheek House"—1958.
- Don Wade Swimming Pool—June 14, 1959.
- Oak Hill School (OHS)—1961; out of attempts or proposals to create more grades for the school came the beginnings of Brentwood Academy and Franklin Road Academy; eventually became K-6th institution.
- Beckerath Organ built in the renovated balcony—1974.
- Family Life Center (gymnasium)—1974.

- Church offices, OHS Library, connector to Education Building—1985–86.
- Columbarium for the interment of ashes—1992; enlarged twice since.
- Connolly-Bryant School of Hope occupies Tyne House—1992–95.
- A Wing and B Wing for OHS and Sunday School, OHS office—2001.
- Limestone Military Memorial Monument Installed in Front of Cheek House—2006.
- Purchase of 801 Robertson Academy Road—2007 (the Sumner property).
- Ministry Wing (administration), new OHS Library, Enrichment Center, relocated swimming pool—2007–2008.
- Purchase of 850 Tyne Boulevard—2010.
- During the 2020–2022 Covid-19 pandemic: slate replaced carpet in the Sanctuary; cameras, lighting, painting, and furniture moving enabled high-quality livestreaming of worship services; major factory-directed maintenance of Beckerath organ performed.

FIRST PRESBYTERIAN CHURCH 91

Church steeple under construction, 1957. Courtesy of First Presbyterian Church of Nashville Archives.

First Presbyterian Church of Nashville's old swimming pool (1959). Courtesy of First Presbyterian Church of Nashville Archives.

Riding ring. The Robertson Academy and Scout building are in background. Courtesy of First Presbyterian Church of Nashville Archives.

Church office entrance after 1985-86 building campaign. Courtesy of First Presbyterian Church of Nashville Archives.

FIRST PRESBYTERIAN CHURCH 93

Armed Forces Memorial in Front of Stanford Chapel. Courtesy of First Presbyterian Church of Nashville Archives.

First Presbyterian Church certificate. For the 1999 Bicentennial of Travellers Rest, "deeds" were sent to current owners of former Travellers Rest property, signed by John Overton, Esq.

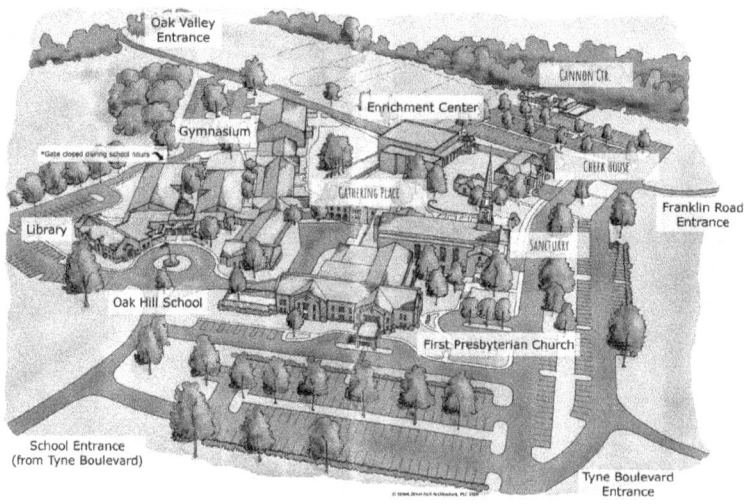

The Campus of First Presbyterian Church and Oak Hill School, 2022. Courtesy of First Presbyterian Church of Nashville.

Chapter Seven

Take a Look Around

The idea of this chapter is that, with our eyes and our imagination, we will take a brief tour of the neighborhood around all sides of the Franklin Road property of First Presbyterian Church. Questions are always asked about "what used to be over there, over here, or back there?" Our little tour should answer some of those questions. We will begin by standing at the big flagpole in front of the church, facing Franklin Road. This flagpole itself has a history; we will start with that story.

The First Presbyterian Church Flagpole

The church flagpole has an inscription: "Harry Hill McAlister III, 1890–1955; Harry Hill McAlister IV, 1922–1944." Hill McAlister IV was a pilot in World War II and was killed in a training accident. The flagpole donation was in memory of this young pilot. The pole was given by brothers Sidney S. McAlister, John David McAlister, and their mother, Marion Stinson McAlister. Sidney and David's father was Hill III. First Presbyterian still has McAlisters, namely Harry Hill McAlister (wife Emily) and his mother, Mary Roberts McAlister. Hill's brother, S. S. McAlister Jr., and sister, Mamie Cayce McAlister, were also in the church for many years. Two things of note: This McAlister family once owned the building on Second Avenue that had housed the Cheek-Neal Coffee Company.[1] This family also owned considerable property along Hogan Road (one traffic light south of First Presbyterian at Franklin Pike. One family house was at 468 Hogan Road, known at times as the Claiborne Place and the House of Seven Gables.[2] The Hogan Road properties were formerly part of Jesse Maxwell's North Carolina land grant. When he secured his preemption for a North Carolina land grant in 1783, Jesse also secured the preemption for Grant #367 for the heirs of David Maxwell, Jesse's brother, who was killed by the Cherokees. Grant #367 became Judge John Overton's Travellers Rest and, eventually, First Presbyterian Church and other entities. The Hogan Road property adjoined the large property that James E. Caldwell had bought from the Pleasant A. Smith family. Son Rogers Caldwell built his Brentwood Hall on his father's property. In 1957, after prolonged litigation, the State of Tennessee took over the Caldwell property, eventually creating the Ellington Agricultural Center, home of the Agriculture Department of the State of Tennessee.

Now, facing Franklin Road, you are looking east. As we go, we will start identifying things around the 360 degrees of a compass face, turning a little bit in a clockwise direction (to the right).

Franklin Road/Franklin Pike

Franklin Road/Franklin Pike (they are the same thing) was the first turnpike in Nashville, connecting, of course, Nashville and Franklin, Tennessee. The Franklin Turnpike Company was incorporated by the state legislature on December 31, 1829. Commissioners appointed by the incorporating act were authorized to sell subscriptions to "shareholders" for the proposed $75,000 project. The pike was to be finished within seven years. Over time, more than a dozen turnpike companies were formed, among them Granny White Turnpike (1850; completed 1855), Owen-Winstead Turnpike (now Edmondson Pike), 1859, and Nolensville Turnpike, about 1837. The Franklin Pike had four toll gates. One was at the Hogan Road and Franklin Pike intersection.[3] When tolls were no longer needed, the toll house was moved up the hill (eastward) and became part of a property and house now owned by First Presbyterian member Admiral Jerry Breast.[4] "Pikes," it should be noted, were little more than hard earth paths mixed with small rocks or gravel. From a historical perspective, Franklin Pike came straight through Judge John Overton's Travellers Rest property, likely following an existing path to Franklin. Older such paths tended to follow buffalo paths. First Presbyterian Church of Nashville Archives has a copy of a contract signed by the landowners through whose lands the new turnpike was traversing. From 1909–1942, the Nashville & Franklin Interurban Railway had streetcars running along Franklin Road. At the point of the church property, the streetcars were on the east side of the road.

Many people have wondered about the origin of the beautiful stone wall along Franklin Road. There is no particularly entertaining story about the wall; they are common all around Nashville. Since they were constructed without mortar, they are called dry-stacked walls. Some walls around Nashville seem to be farmer-built, assembled by simply piling up stones dug up in plowing. Even today, anyone who has tried to establish gardens in this area understands that all of Middle Tennessee has layers of limestone close to the ground's surface. As they piled up, no doubt the owners decided to use the stones to mark boundaries or corral livestock. The more professional-looking fences one sees, such as First Presbyterian's, are the handiwork of stone masons, no doubt using the labor of enslaved persons. In 2008, the Historical Commission of Metropolitan Nashville and Davidson County erected Historical Marker #132 on Granny White Pike between Sewanee Road and Gateway Lane. This marker tells of just such a wall as First Presbyterian's. The marker reads:

> Dry-stack stone walls, a Scots-Irish building tradition adapted by slaves in the early 19th century, were common throughout Middle Tennessee. During the 1864 Battle of Nashville, Brigadier General Henry Jackson was captured at this wall on the Middle Franklin Turnpike after the Confederate line collapsed at Shy's Hill. [Middle Franklin Pike was the earlier name of Granny White Pike].

The First Presbyterian wall could have been built by the Travellers Rest Overtons after the Franklin Turnpike was constructed in the 1830s to keep travelers off the Overtons' west acreage. If it had been built as late as the late 1880s by Van Leer Kirkman, it would not have been made by enslaved persons. However, it is known that enslaved persons who learned the trade became masons themselves, adding that skill, which was continued in their descendants.

John Overton High School

Directly across Franklin Road is John Overton High School. All of the property that is the school was once part of Travellers Rest, just as the First Presbyterian property was. The property was willed to Col. John Overton's child, Martha M. Overton Dickinson, when he died in 1898. The property was handed down in the family and eventually left the family. Davidson County Schools acquired the property in 1957,[5] and John Overton High School was opened in 1958, with seventh and eighth grades only. A dedication event was held on April 5, 1959. The first Principal was Edmond Tipton, and the eighth graders became the first graduating class in 1963. At one time, much of this land was owned by John H. and Susan Glenn Cheek, who had obtained it from the Dickinson family, heirs to the Overton family. The Cheeks sold this property in 1941, long before a school was imagined for the land.

Judson Baptist Church

Judson Baptist Church was founded in 1911, but not at today's location. It was much closer to downtown Nashville, just off 8th Avenue on Prentice Avenue. Judson was the second church in the Waverly Place subdivision; Glen Leven Presbyterian was the first. A small piece of the former building is still there, now part of the Gruhn Guitars building. The church bought the current property in 1964 and opened its doors for worship in 1969.[6] All of the Judson property was also part of Travellers Rest. A new Sanctuary was built in 1980.[7]

Holy Trinity Greek Orthodox Church

Turning to the right again, you are facing two houses that face Tyne Boulevard. Beyond these houses lies the large acreage that is home to Holy Trinity Greek Orthodox Church. This property was also Overton until it was subdivided in 1920, becoming the Overton Park Subdivision.[8] The previous house on this large property was called

Beauvoir, the 1926 home built by Mrs. Jesse Maxwell Overton. This property is now the site of Holy Trinity Greek Orthodox Church. From History of Homes and Gardens of Tennessee. Courtesy of Tennessee State Library and Archives.

Beauvoir, built in 1925–1926 by Sarah "Saidee" Williams Overton. Sarah was the widow of Jesse Maxwell Overton, son of Col. John Overton. Jesse and Saidee had built an estate home named Overton Hall on some Travellers Rest land at what is now the intersection of Stillwood Drive and Crieve Road. Saidee sold that property in 1925 to Herbert and Helen Ritchey Cheek Farrell. The Farrells changed the name of Overton Hall to Crieve Hall. Those 433 acres eventually became part of today's Crieve Hall neighborhood. The house was not far from today's Crieve Hall Elementary School. Saidee Overton lived at Beauvoir with her daughter, Elizabeth Williams Overton Colton, and Elizabeth's husband, Henry Elliott Colton. Elizabeth and Henry's four children were also living at Beauvoir. This home was sold in 1936 to Margaret Grooms Ragland, then to John W. and Edna Gunn Little in 1949. The Littles sold it in 1961 to Robertson and Patricia Potter McDonald. Holy Trinity Greek Orthodox Church bought the property in 1977.[9] The church began holding worship and activities on the 13.5-acre property in 1986; a Sanctuary was built and was first occupied in 1992. This congregation had previously been on 6th Avenue in Nashville, at one of the former locations of the Wallace School of Nashville.[10] The stone entrance structure on Franklin Road, very near Tyne Boulevard, was the driveway to Beauvoir.[11]

Tyne Boulevard

This long street was not always a continuous road from Franklin Road to Hillsboro Pike. Over time, it evolved in pieces. The part from Franklin Road westward for an undetermined length was known as LeaLand Road, clearly labeled as such when the Overton subdivision in 1920 was accomplished, yielding many lots on the south side of the road and Franklin Road.[12] A nearby major road today bears the name Lealand Lane, preserving the Lea family connection in the Oak Hill area. Tyne was named for Thomas J. Tyne, one of the founders of the National Life and Accident Insurance Company.[13] Tyne's estate was at what is now Hillsboro Road and Tyne Boulevard, a striking property that still has land, water, and cattle. Thomas Tyne's daughter, Catherine Jane Tyne, became the second wife of Edward Potter Jr. (see "The Treemont Development on Tyne" below). Two lots directly across Tyne Boulevard from First Presbyterian's street entrance nearest Franklin Road were owned briefly by Dr. Walter Rowe Courtenay, former pastor of First Presbyterian Church, about the time the congregation moved to Franklin Road from downtown. Courtenay sold the lots to Gladys Stahlman in 1956.[14]

The Treemont Development on Tyne

Treemont was formerly the home and estate known as Treemont, owned by Edward Potter Jr. Of course, the land traces back to Travellers Rest, as does everything in the neighborhood. Treemont is part of the Overton property subdivided as Overton Park in 1920, the large subdivision that gave rise to the Holy Trinity Greek Orthodox Church property. Edward Potter Jr. was the founder of the Commerce Union Bank of Nashville, originally known as the German American Bank, later as the Farmers & Merchants Bank. Potter was married to Bertha Herbert, then to Catherine Tyne after Bertha's death.

Potter died in 1976.[15] His daughters, Jean Potter McCann and Patricia Potter McDonald, eventually sold the property for development. The current Treemont development, containing fifty-one lots, was developed in 1986.[16] Patricia and Robertson McDonald were the same people who last owned Beauvoir on Franklin Road before it was sold to Holy Trinity Greek Orthodox Church. Edward Potter's successor at Commerce Union was William F. Earthman Jr., whose first wife was Alice Tyne. Alice's grandfather was Thomas J. Tyne, the namesake of Tyne Boulevard. One of Earthman's children with Alice Tyne is John Christopher Burch Earthman, a current member of First Presbyterian Church. The regional Boy Scout headquarters building on Hillsboro Pike, the Jet Potter Service Center, was named for Edward Potter's younger brother, Justin "Jet" Potter.

Kirkman Lane/the Bridle Path

Unlike other items on our tour around the perimeter of First Presbyterian Church property, Kirkman Lane is not readily visible. This small lane was established as a passage from Judge John Overton's Travellers Rest estate westward to a part of his property given to his daughter, Elizabeth B. Overton, and her spouse, Judge John M. Lea. They were married in 1843, and their home was on the east side of Middle Franklin Pike, now Granny White Pike. The small pathway began at Travellers Rest and was undoubtedly the driveway leading to Franklin Pike. That part is now Farrell Parkway, becoming Overton Lane across Franklin Pike. Overton Lane no longer goes all the way to Tyne Boulevard, but it used to. It seems that Edward Potter Jr. chose that the lane did not go all the way through his property after he developed his Treemont estate on formerly Overton land on the south side of Tyne Boulevard. The lane was re-routed to the west, lying between what is now the entrance to Treemont and the corner of Tyne Boulevard and Overton Lea Lane. The lane is now quite visible from Tyne Boulevard, where it crosses over and becomes the western property line of 856 Tyne Boulevard and the west boundary of a small part of First Presbyterian Church. The lane then turns left, behind houses on Oak Valley Lane, then northward again after crossing Robertson Academy Road. Crossing

Lealand Lane in a westward direction, the lane once went all the way to Granny White Pike. It no longer goes that far, but a small spur turns northward at about Robin Springs Road.

One must remember that almost none of the mentioned roads existed when the lane began as Overton Lane. The road simply connected Travellers Rest with the Leas on Granny White Pike (Middle Franklin Pike.) A slave-built stone wall was built in the 1840s, and a significant part of the lane went right next to that wall. The wall marked the boundary between Overtons and Leas. That wall is still very visible in the Lealand-Sewanee-Stonewall neighborhood. A map in the church archives from 1878 clearly shows the entire length of the lane. At various times, the lane has been called Overton Lane, Lea Lane, Kirkman Lea Avenue, and Kirkman Lane. Many modern maps still show Kirkman Lane on them, though it has never been approved as a public thoroughfare. Informally, a particular stretch of the lane became known to residents as the Bridle Path, a safe place for children and others to ride horses. After Robertson Academy was moved in 1912 to its present location and Robertson Academy Road was created, neighborhood students rode their ponies to school there.

In the Civil War, the old stone wall played a significant role in the 1864 Battle of Nashville. Today, a historical marker placed in 1967 marks the area where Kirkman Lane and the wall intersect. On December 16, 1864, it was there that retreating Confederate troops used the wall as temporary protection against advancing Federal troops. Eventually, defensive lines were broken, and the Confederate forces continued retreating to Brentwood and southward to Alabama. Judge John M. Lea was Nashville's mayor some years before the Civil War. He was a "Unionist" during the war but was helpful afterward in helping Confederate veterans regain their voting rights. Judge Lea's son, Overton Lea, inherited the western estate from him and built the notable Lealand home on the 1200 acres of that property.

Why was the lane eventually called Kirkman Lane? In 1887, Van Leer Kirkman bought sixty-four-plus acres of land (today's First Presbyterian property) from Col. John Overton and several hundred more acres of the former Barton land grant. Most of Overton Lane was on Kirkman property, with the natural consequence that people called it Kirkman's Lane.

The narrow lane was never declared a public road for unclear reasons, but it still exists, primarily as backyard boundaries. Just south of Battery Lane, one small part was the subject of numerous neighborhood meetings in the 1970s as developers sought to build duplexes on Kirkman Lane near Sewanee Road. Newspapers of the day covered these discussions between City of Oak Hill residents and would-be developers.[17]

850 Tyne Boulevard

This five-acre property, immediately adjacent to First Presbyterian's Tyne House, was part of the Van Leer Kirkman purchase of sixty-four acres of the Travellers Rest property in 1887. The five acres became a separate property when Susan Anderson Cheek married William Howard Eason in 1941. Her parents, John H. and Susan Glenn Cheek, gave these newlyweds that part of their property. The property eventually had several owners, and, in 2010, First Presbyterian Church bought it. The house itself was never used by the church and was eventually razed. A garage apartment was used by the church for a time, including the use by one of the church's organists, but it, too, was eventually torn down. At publication time, First Presbyterian Church, Oak Hill School, and the City of Oak Hill are exploring the possibility of athletic facilities being created on that part of church property. In 2021, the property was legally consolidated into First Presbyterian Church property.[18] Church members John Eason and the late William Howard Eason Jr. grew up in the house at 850 Tyne Boulevard.

Oak Hill Valley Subdivision

Once you exit the back (west) entrance of the church property, you find yourself in a subdivision, the property that the church did not buy from the Cheek family in 1949. That option was for about 165 acres, all part of the former Kirkman Oak Hill farm. The Cheek family sold the property in August 1950 to the Oak Hill Land Company. That entity created a subdivision of 119 building lots, officially known as

John Cheek Eason is the only remaining blood-related Cheek left in First Presbyterian Church. He is an Elder at the church. The photo was taken in 2020. Courtesy of First Presbyterian Church of Nashville Archives.

This property/house at 850 Tyne Boulevard was the 1941 wedding gift when Susan Anderson Cheek married William Howard Eason. The five-acre property was part of the larger John Hancock Cheek estate. Three children grew up in the house, including William Howard Eason Jr. and John Cheek Eason. The church owns the property now and has razed the house. Photo by author.

Oak Hill Valley Subdivision.[19] The streets designed for the subdivision were Oak Valley Lane, Van Leer Drive, Churchwood Drive, and Dustin Lane; Robertson Academy Road was extended beyond the school to the end of the subdivision.

Robertson Academy School

When one stands facing the front of the Cannon Youth Center of First Presbyterian Church, another building looms in the background, looking very much like part of the church property. It is not, in fact, on the church campus. The building is Robertson Academy, whose historical roots make it the oldest public school in Davidson County.

The construction of Robertson Academy was authorized by the Tennessee General Assembly in an 1806 act creating public academies in each of the twenty-seven counties of that time. The United States government had recently ceded land to the states for the purpose of setting up schools. The 1806 Tennessee act provided for trustees to be appointed to operate the school, said trustees to have "perpetual succession." Robertson Academy's original trustees were Thomas A. Claiborne, Joel Lewis, Robert Weakley, Joseph Phillips, and Robert Foster. Trustees added in 1911, when the original act was modified, were William Williams, William Donelson, John Harden, and John Anderson.

Further amendments in 1817 and 1840 provided county courts with the power to appoint trustees. In 1841, the Davidson County Court appointed James F. May, Jesse Maxwell, William H. Phillips, Robert Scales, William Hartsfield, John Hogan, and John Thompson. The original land was bought in 1842 for five dollars in a quitclaim from William Hartsfield to the Trustees for "an acre" of the Hartsfield land bordering Jesse Maxwell's land and William Ewing's land. Trustee Jesse Maxwell granted free use of a spring to the school.[20] This location of the school is not today's Robertson Academy location. The 1842 location was east of Franklin Pike, near what is now the intersection of Blackman Road and Salem Drive.

The 1842 land donation/sale by William Hartsfield brings up questions about who actually provided the land for the early Robertson

Academy. Maxwell family lore holds that Jesse Maxwell gave an acre or so in 1806 or 1807 for this purpose. Nashville historian Ridley Wills II notes this family belief in his *Nashville Pikes 1*, citing Mary Maxwell (Mollie) Claiborne's family memoir.[21] Legal research done in 1911 by E. L. McNeilly and the 1842 quitclaim deed itself seems to give authoritative clarification that Hartsfield gave the land. The McNeilly research holds that Jesse Maxwell's only contribution was to give the school access to spring water from his land.[22] Since the Hartsfield property shared a boundary with the Maxwell property, it also seems possible that in those early days, the boundaries were not clearly mapped and what was once Maxwell land might have ended up later being Hartsfield land. It is hard to find a definitive answer here.

The First Presbyterian Church Archives has a copy of an interesting 1897 map that shows the little acre, clearly marked "Robertson Academy." This map shows the subdivision into parts of the lands of Pleasant A. Smith.[23] The school plot is on the Smith property, on the boundary of the Thomas Claiborne property. Claiborne had married into the Maxwell family, so it is quite probable that Claiborne lands were those formerly called Maxwell lands. The huge Smith property is the same as that previously owned by William Hartsfield, and before him, by William Ewing, who received a North Carolina Land Grant in that area. All the Smith lands were eventually bought by James E. Caldwell, a First Presbyterian Church member. Caldwell owned the Cumberland Telephone Company in the early 1900s, as well as the Glendale Park amusement park. Caldwell's son, Rogers Caldwell, built his Brentwood Hall mansion in 1927–28 on a part of this land we are discussing. Eventually, the State of Tennessee took over most of the land, now Ellington Agricultural Center and Metro Nashville's Whitfield Park.[24]

A previous paragraph said that Robertson Academy was near the present-day intersection of Blackman Road and Salem Drive. Blackman Road is a long and main artery today, connecting the I-65/Harding Place exit area with Edmondson Pike. Blackman Road marks the northern boundary of the large property we are discussing. Dr. Blackman was a sugar cane planter from Louisiana who owned extensive property in the South Davidson County area, along with neighbor landowners Andrew Ewing, Daniel Hogan, a Mr. Edmiston, Jesse Maxwell, and John Overton. Hogan is said to have been the first teacher at Robertson Academy. Today's Hogan Road, which connects Franklin Pike with the Ellington Agricultural Center and Edmondson Pike, runs along part of Daniel Hogan's former lands. A small cemetery still in existence on the Ellington Agricultural Center property holds the graves of William Ewing, Pleasant A. Smith, and William Hartsfield, along with many family members.

The original Robertson Academy was said to be a log structure used until just before the Civil War when it was replaced by a substantial brick structure still standing on the estate of Rogers Caldwell in 1925.[25] The old school eventually burned after moving to the Robertson Academy Road location.

History tells us that the trustees were such staunch supporters of the school that during the Civil War—when student travel to school was a dangerous activity due to military action in the area—the academy was temporarily relocated to Travellers Rest, closer to the homes of several of the students. Mrs. Thomas Claiborne (née Ann Maxwell) stayed at Travellers Rest while her husband was in the Army. She taught her children and any neighborhood children who could get there. During that time, the school's horses were put out of service so as not to tempt Union military procurement parties roaming the district. Robertson Academy supplied horses for its students. The school system—or the State Legislature—was not keen on giving public funds for horse feed and expenses, so the trustees and parents kept up the horse part of the children's education.[26]

There is a very puzzling piece of Robertson Academy's history. A report of the Robertson Academy Trustees to the Tennessee General Assembly dated 1824 indicates that the school did not get underway until the 1820s. Unfortunately, that is the only report of its nature to be found in Metro Nashville or State Archives.[27]

A document called *History of Robertson Academy* by school alumnus James Casper Norris Jr. is another mystery. Though it is mentioned in historical newspaper articles, including a 1935 *Nashville Banner* piece,

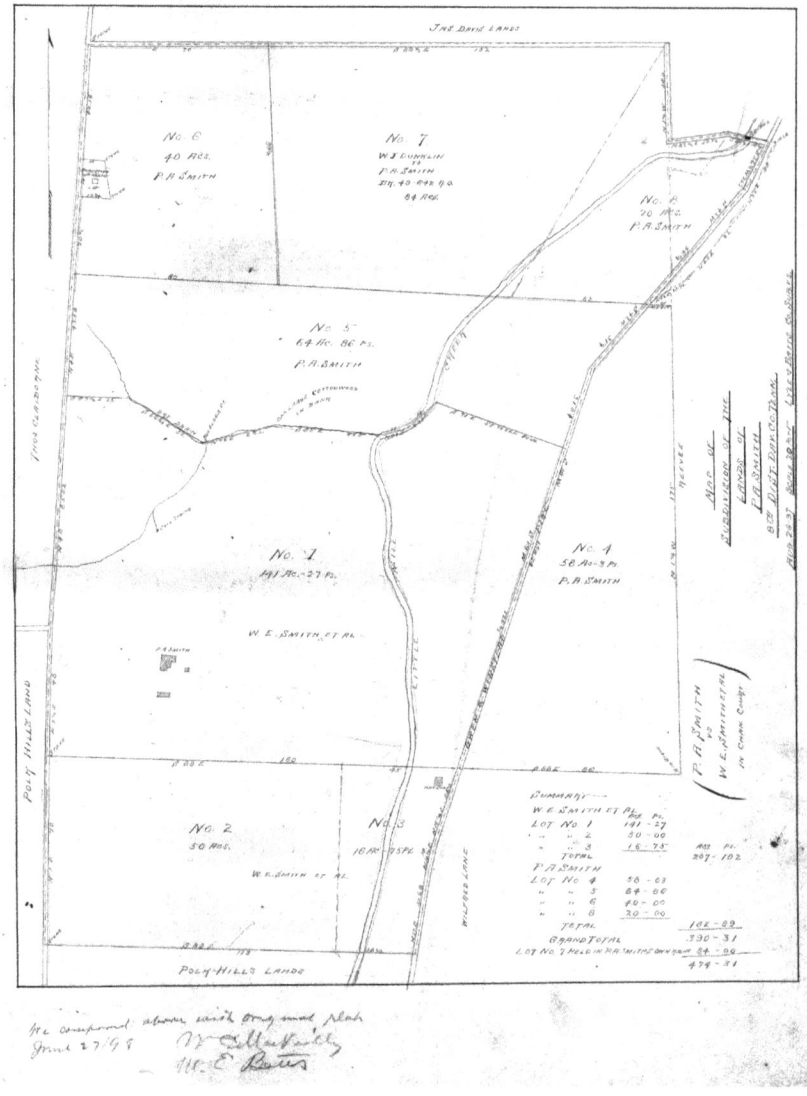

The 1897 Subdivision of Pleasant A. Smith property, showing the old location of Robertson Academy. P. A. Smith and his relatives are buried in a cemetery located in one of the lots which now comprise the Ellington Agricultural Center of the Tennessee State Department of Agriculture. James E. Caldwell eventually owned all of the Smith lots; son Rogers Caldwell built his "Brentwood Hall" on the property. Map from *Davidson County Plan Book 2*, 68. Courtesy of Metro Nashville Archives.

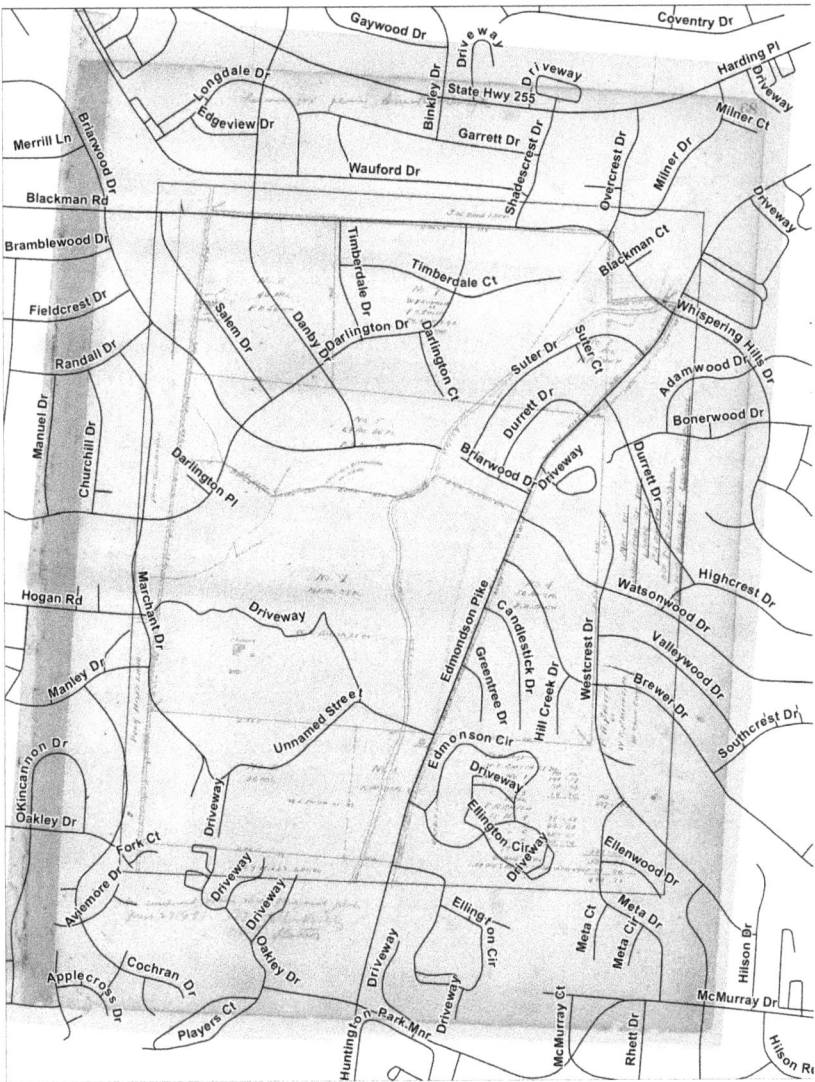

Overlay of the 1897 Subdivision of Pleasant A. Smith property. Courtesy of Philip McGavock Morrissey, Tennessee Dept. of Agriculture, Forestry Division.

the author has never been able to locate this elusive work, which, if found, could be very valuable in solving some of the aforementioned mysteries.[28]

Robertson Academy moved to its present location after its Trustees were gifted in 1911 with about two acres of land by Mrs. Mary McConnell "Con" Overton Thompson. Her land inheritance from the death of her father, Col. John Overton, in 1898, was on the west side of Franklin Pike. The Robert Jones sale (next section) and the Robertson Academy gift came from her larger inheritance. Her land stretched northward from the Van Leer Kirkman Oak Hill farm. The Thompsons lived at Glen Leven Farm, operated by Mrs. Thompson's husband, John Thompson. The new Robertson Academy was built in 1912–1913 and burned in 1932. The present school was completed in 1933 and has had additions several times since then. The school is still part of the Metropolitan Nashville Public Schools system.

The Sumner Property

The house and lot at 801 Robertson Academy Road, long known at First Presbyterian Church as the Sumner property, is owned by First Presbyterian. The church bought it on October 31, 2007, from the children of Billy T. and Sue W. Sumner, both longtime members of the church. However, the property's history goes back nearly a century before the church purchase, and there was a church connection even then.

When Van Leer Kirkman bought sixty-four acres of Col. John Overton's Franklin Road-facing Travellers Rest property in 1887, the land adjoining the northern boundary of Kirkman's purchase remained Overton property. From that boundary northward became the horse-raising enterprise known as Hermitage Stud. Neither Robertson Academy nor Robertson Academy Road was in existence then. At Colonel Overton's 1898 death, about 133 acres of that land north of Van Leer Kirkman and west of Franklin Road was inherited by Overton's daughter, Mary McConnell "Con" Overton Thompson. She had married John M. Thompson, also known as John Thompson Jr., a notable family along Franklin Road. John Jr.'s father had built the Glen Leven house and estate farther north along Franklin Road. Van

Leer Kirkman's wife, Katherine Thompson Kirkman, was related to those Thompsons. Con and John Jr. lived in the Glen Leven house. Glen Leven still stands on a small part of the large estate and is now owned and controlled by the Land Trust of Tennessee.

In 1910, Mrs. Thompson sold approximately 4.87 acres of her west-of-Franklin Road land to Robert Franklin Jones.[29] The sale was made for $2,435. The Davidson County Chancery Court minutes show that the land was "unimproved at this time." The court was urged to approve the sale because it would enhance the value of the land for both parties "by reason of the building and operation of the Nashville Interurban Railroad, running along the East side of the Nashville and Franklin Turnpike," immediately across the street from both properties. It was stated that farming would no longer be in the best interests of all and that land along that corridor would best be developed and sold "by careful sales in small tracts or parcels for residential purposes."[30] The property in question ran 250 feet along Franklin Road, then 850 feet westward, with 250 and 850 feet on the other sides forming a rectangular lot. Kirkman property formed the southern boundary of the lot. John Thompson and Joseph H. Thompson oversaw "depositions in pursuit of the sale."[31] These two men are the same brothers whose names are on a silver baptismal bowl at First Presbyterian Church. Their mother, this same Con Thompson, gave the bowl at the time of their baptism in 1854.

Not long after this purchase of Thompson land, the same Mrs. Thompson donated about 2 acres of adjoining land in 1911 to the Trustees of Robertson Academy, then located a few miles east of Franklin Road, for the purpose of enabling Robertson Academy to relocate. Robertson Academy did move, and a school was built in 1912–1913 on its current spot. Robertson Academy Road was created to give access to the new school. Again, the southern boundary for the Jones and Robertson Academy properties was the Van Leer Kirkman property, which became First Presbyterian Church property. That boundary is still the same.

On May 6, 1942, Ralph Franklin Jones transferred ownership of his 250' x 850' property to his son Ralph Culbert Jones, including the house the father had built. The transaction was a "life estate" type of deed.³² The Jones house was finished in 1910. The original entrance to the property was from Franklin Road, through stone pillars, still visible today near the Robertson Academy Road corner. The driveway went left from the entrance, then along the Kirkman property line, to the house and a porte-cochère on the north side of the house, allowing for the departure of passengers from carriages and automobiles. The porte-cochère eventually became a screened porch, then an enclosed sunroom.³³

On April 20, 1959, Billy T. Sumner and Sue W. Sumner bought the Jones property from Ralph C. and Margaret M. Jones. By then, or shortly after, the property was described as "Lots 1 and 2 of the Ralph C. Jones Subdivision." Lot 2 was the rear lot, approximately 2.8 acres, with its west boundary as the Robertson Academy property. Lot 1, fronting on Franklin Road, was about 2.1 acres. Billy Sumner, a partner in Barge, Waggoner, and Sumner, did the surveying himself. Lot 1, known eventually as 4801 Franklin Road, was sold on August 3, 1959, to Umberto Marchetti, passing to his daughter, Sandra Marchetti Click, on July 29, 1994. Lot 2, with the house, was sold to First Presbyterian Church on October 31, 2007, by Sumner's daughters, Kim Sumner Hardin and Shellie Sumner Unger.

Zoning restrictions of the City of Oak Hill have prevented First Presbyterian Church from using the Sumner house, as it is referred to, for ministry events calling for groups to gather and park. As a result, the house has had long periods of disuse or underuse. Executive Pastor Sam Cooper and his wife Lily lived in the house from July 2010 to July 2017, and Associate Pastor Joshua Rodriguez and his family occupied the place in 2017. In 2021, the property was legally incorporated into the First Presbyterian Church's main property. Speculation has always existed about the possibility or desirability of First Presbyterian purchasing Lot 1 of the original property; persistent flooding of the property is likely one deterrent. In 2022 First Presbyterian used the house for its Room in the Inn program.

Franklin Road Academy

The last stop on our "Take a Look Around" journey is that of the Franklin Road Academy (FRA), whose long property stretches along Franklin Road from Harding Place all the way to John Overton High School (OHS). Like everything in the neighborhood, all the property was part of Travellers Rest, the plantation estate of Judge John Overton and then his son Col. John Overton. Eventually, a son of Colonel Overton, May Overton, inherited Overton lands on the East side of Franklin Pike; farther down the line, the property left the family. These acres included the former peach orchard of Travellers Rest, destined to become famous in the Civil War, when the struggle for Peach Orchard Hill was a bloody second-day feature of the Battle of Nashville in December 1864. Part of that battle area is now the part of Harding Place leading to and including the southbound on-ramp to Interstate 65. The future FRA home began with the purchase by the First Christian Church of Nashville of acreage along Franklin Pike, that acreage being the part nearest John Overton High School. The church itself was formed in 1953 as a split or outgrowth of Vine Street Christian Church in downtown Nashville. The congregation bought some property on Franklin Road in 1958, for $40,000, from the Wehby family.[34]

    A confluence of events led to the 1971 beginning of Franklin Road Academy. The decision across the street at First Presbyterian's Oak Hill School not to grow itself beyond the sixth grade led OHS Business Manager and teacher Bill Bradshaw to pursue just such a school plan in another location. A former OHS Head of School, Bill Brown, had previously left Oak Hill School for the same reason; thus, Brentwood Academy came into being. Bradshaw approached the officers of First Christian Church with a proposal for a school on their property. The church was of a mind to extend its ministry in new directions; the partnership was formed. Bonds were sold, many to First Christian Church members, and the groundbreaking was on May 23, 1971. The new school year began on September 13. The school came into being only six months after the Bradshaw proposal to the church officers! Many church members served as faculty and staff at the school, and both school and church benefitted from the shared use of existing and new buildings. Eventually, as the school grew and the church began to lose members, the partnership grew more complicated, and, in 2005, the church moved out. FRA bought the buildings. First Christian Church eventually ended up in Franklin, Tennessee, where it took the name Aspen Grove Christian Church.

Appendix A: How the Glen Leven Farm Thompsons and Oak Hill Farm Kirkmans Were Related

Time and time again, while doing the research for this book, I got so lost in family connections that I had to stop and piece together charts such as this one. The Maxwells, Overtons, Claibornes, Thompsons, Kirkmans, Caldwells, Cheeks, and other families, all have interesting and complicated histories. How they overlap repeatedly is a fascinating part of the history of the south Davidson County area described in this current book.

1. Van Leer Kirkman, owner of the Oak Hill estate, was married to Katherine "Kate" Thompson, daughter of Macon Caswell Thompson.
2. Macon's father (Kate's grandfather) was Jacob Thompson, who was married to Catherine A. Jones Thompson.
3. Jacob's father was Nicholas Thompson, who was married to Lucretia Van Hook Thompson.
4. Nicholas was brother to Ann Thompson, who was called "Nancy."
5. Ann (Nancy) Thompson married a Thomas Thompson. Ann's parents and Thomas's parents were from Orange County, North Carolina; family historians can't prove conclusively whether or not Ann and Thomas were cousins.
6. One of Thomas and Nancy's children was John Thompson.
7. John Thompson built the house today known as Glen Leven on Franklin Road; other houses he built on the site burned.

8. John Thompson had four wives; the fourth was Mary Hamilton House Thompson. One of their several children—John M., known also as John Jr.—married into the neighboring Overton family of Travellers Rest.

9. So, Kate Thompson Kirkman's family line goes back to Nicholas and Lucretia Van Hook Thompson. The Glen Leven Thompsons go back to Ann (Nancy), the sister of Nicholas Thompson.

10. The parents of Nicholas and Nancy were Joseph and Sarah McAlister/McAllister Thompson; you would say that the common ancestors were Joseph and Sarah Thompson.

11. Joseph's parents were Thomas Thompson and Ann Finney Thompson. The Thompson family begins its family tree with this Thomas Thompson (died 1795) of Pennsylvania, then of Orange County, North Carolina. Thomas Thompson was awarded a Land Grant in Middle Tennessee for his Revolutionary War service. A neighboring land grant was that secured for "the heirs of David Maxwell." The Maxwell grant became Judge John Overton's Travellers Rest, a part of which was destined to become the First Presbyterian Church Franklin Pike/Oak Hill property.

Appendix B: The Pastors of 4815 Franklin Road

Six ministers have served as Pastor/Head of Staff since First Presbyterian Church moved from downtown Nashville to the Oak Hill/Franklin Road property in 1955. Numerous Assistant and Associate Pastors, and Pastoral Associates, have also served at the suburban location. The six men who have served as pastor at the Franklin Road location are pictured below and on the next three pages.

Walter Rowe Courtenay, first pastor, 1944–1971. Courtesy of First Presbyterian Church of Nashville.

118   Appendix B

Cortez Cooper, second pastor, 1971–1981. Courtesy of First Presbyterian Church of Nashville.

William T. Bryant, third pastor, 1981–1994. Courtesy of First Presbyterian Church of Nashville.

Appendix B

Thomas Tyndall, fourth pastor, 1996–2000. Courtesy of First Presbyterian Church of Nashville.

Todd B. Jones, fifth pastor, 2002–2019. Courtesy of First Presbyterian Church of Nashville.

Ryan V. Moore, sixth pastor, 2019 to-date. Courtesy of First Presbyterian Church of Nashville.

Appendix C: Text of North Carolina Land Grant #367

The following paragraph with indented text represents the document on the cover of *Out Franklin Road* as officially recorded by the State of North Carolina in 1794. It is also shown at the end of this appendix. This Land Grant began its life as a "preemption" issued to Jesse Maxwell on January 16, 1783, in the name of "the Heirs of David Maxwell." David Maxwell was Jesse's late brother. Throughout the handwritten court document, Maxwell is rendered as "Maxell." Since this is prior to Tennessee's 1796 entry as a state, the County of Davidson is still a North Carolina county. A "pole" is a unit of measurement used by surveyors. In 1794, Richard Dobbs Spaight was Governor of North Carolina; James Glasgow was North Carolina's first Secretary of State.

> William Maxell and Moses Maxell May 13, 1794
> Territory of the United States State of North Carolina
> No. 367
>
> To all to whom these presents shall come, Greeting. Know ye that we for and in consideration of the sum of ten pounds for every hundred acres hereby granted paid into our Treasury by William Maxell and Moses Maxell, have given and granted and by these presents do give and grant to Messrs. William Maxell and Moses Maxell a tract of land containing six hundred and forty acres lying and being in the County of Davidson on the waters of the West fork of Mill Creek. Beginning at a Sugar sapling on William Simpson's West boundary, running thence with Jesse Maxell's line South forty five degrees West, two hundred poles to a Sugar tree and Box Elder, West one hundred and ninety two poles to a Sugar tree, North three hundred and thirty four poles to a Black Oak, East three hundred and thirty five poles to a Dogwood in

Simpson's West boundary. South one hundred ninety four poles with Simpson's line to the beginning. With all woods, waters, mines, minerals, hereditaments and appurtenances to the said land belonging or appertaining. To hold to Messrs. William Maxell and Moses Maxell, their heirs and assigns forever. Which land was surveyed for Messrs. Maxells January 25th, 1785, by James Mulherin, DS, in consequence of a Warrant No. 112, entered January 15th, 1784.

This Grant signed Richard Dobbs Spaight, with Seal of the State affixed, June 26th, 1793; countersigned J. Glasgow, Sec'y.

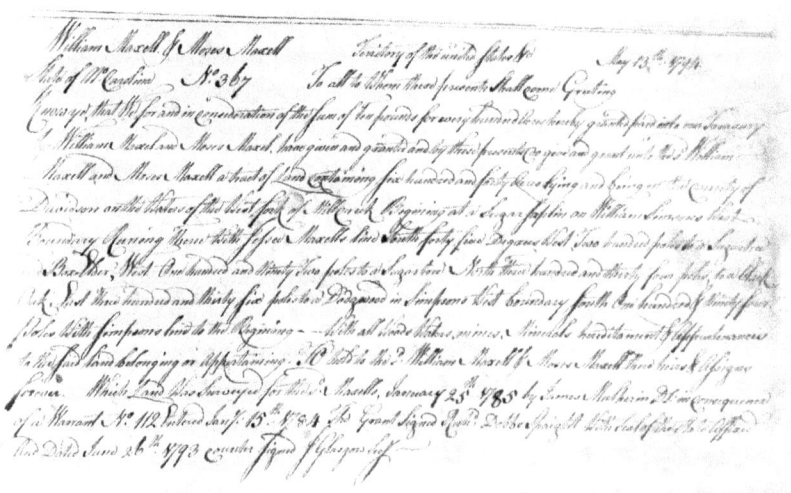

Notes

Chapter One
Prior to Tennessee Statehood

1. Information for this chapter section comes from several sources:
   - https://www.mountvernon.org, accessed January 18, 2022.
   - https://www.history.com/topics/native-american-history/french-and-indian-war, accessed January 18, 2022.
   - https://www.totallyhistory.com/french-and-indian-war, accessed January 18, 2022.
   - https://www.britannica.com/event/French-and-Indian-War, accessed January 18, 2022.

2. Dr. Carole Bucy, Davidson County, TN Historian, emphasizes this in her "Nashville 101" public lectures. The author attended these lectures in April 2019.

3. Wilma Dykeman, *Tennessee, A Bicentennial History* (Nashville, TN: American Association for State and Local History, 1975), 42.

4. Max Dixon, Introduction to *The Wataugans* (Johnson City, TN: The Overmountain Press, 1989).

5. Ibid., 16.

6. Harriette Arnow, *Seedtime on the Cumberland* (New York: Macmillan Co., 1960), 60ff.

7. Many dramatic speeches are said to have been made at Sycamore Shoals. The fiery Dragging Canoe ... "dramatically jumped into a discussion circle ... pointed to the West ... and shouted, 'There is a dark cloud hanging over that country—it is a dark and bloody ground. You will pay a heavy price if you take it from us.'" This proved to be true, and Dragging Canoe himself was the chief instrument of fulfillment of the prophecy and threat against settlement of Kentucky and the Cumberland area. But the treaty was signed on March 17, 1775. Mary French Caldwell, *Tennessee: The Dangerous Example: Watauga to 1849* (Knoxville, TN: Aurora Publications, 1974).

8. "A Memorable Day in the History of Nashville," *Nashville Daily American*, April 25, 1880. The largest parade in Nashville history went from downtown to the State

Capitol. Bands floats, veterans' organizations, and fire engines were in abundance. Various "industries" of the city were represented by 204 decorated wagons. Veterans and other units made sure to pause and salute Mrs. James K. Polk at her Vine Street residence; President Polk was at that time still interred on that property. The Polks were parishioners at First Presbyterian Church. The church's pastor, the Rev. Dr. Thomas A. Hoyt, delivered the "Centennial Prayer" from the stage at the Capitol. The prayer was printed in the newspapers.

9. Memorial Erected to Nashville's Founders," *Nashville Tennessean*, April 25, 1910.

10. Irene M. Griffey, *The Preemptors: Tennessee's First Settlers* (Clarksville, TN: I. M. Griffey, 1989), 15.

11. Ibid., Preface.

12. Ibid.

13. Griffey, Preface.

14. Mary Maxwell (Mollie) Claiborne, *A History of the Jesse Maxwell Family in Tennessee* (Nashville, TN: unpublished manuscript, 1929), 18.

15. Griffey, 15.

16. Jack Masters, Bill Puryear, *Founding of the Cumberland Settlements: The Second Atlas, 1779–1804* (Gallatin, TN: Warioto Press, 2011), 41. The authors quote a source which lists all who fought at Kings Mountain.

17. —Claiborne, 3–4. Claiborne goes on to say that "it is highly probable that David Maxwell (Jesse's father, not brother) may be buried in Augusta or Albemarle County, Va." It seems unlikely to the author that if Jesse's father had anything to do with the Tennessee experience, he would have been brought back to Virginia for burial.

18 Doug Drake, Jack Martin, and Bill Puryear, *Founding of the Cumberland Settlements: The First Atlas, 1779–1804* (Gallatin, TN: Warioto Press, 2009), 110.

19. Claiborne, 10.

Chapter Two

The Overton Years

1. Henry Lee Swint, "Travellers Rest: Home of Judge John Overton," *Tennessee Historical Quarterly*, xxvi (Spring 1967): 6.

2. Nan Overton West, compiler, *The Overtons: 700 Years*, 1998.

3. Kenneth P'Pool, *John Overton: Landowner and Developer* (unpublished paper, 1978), 1. Kenneth P'Pool was Deputy State Historic Preservation Officer, Mississippi Department of Archives and History.

4. Ibid.

5. Ibid.

6. P'Pool, 2. P'Pool references two sources for historical information on Overton: Swint (above); and Louise Littleton Davis, *Historic Travellers Rest* (Nashville: Travellers Rest, 1976).

7. Davidson County Register of Deeds, Book "D," 62; and Book "E," 393.

8. P'Pool, 5–6, citing Davis, 9 & 11.

9. Swint, 7–8.

10. P'Pool, Appendix with title "Travelers Rest," unnumbered page, based on ROD, Book "S," 83–85, dealing with the "processioning" of Overton's land, circa 1829.

11. P'Pool, 2.

12. Ibid, 8.

13. Swint, 9.

14. Frances Clifton, "John Overton as Andrew Jackson's Friend." *Tennessee Historical Quarterly*, ii, no. 1 (March 1952): 23–40. This quote is from a letter from Judge John Overton to Col. John Overton, February 23, 1824, reprinted in John M. Lea's "Biographical Sketch of Judge John Overton," in *Proceedings of the Tenth Annual Meeting of the Bar Association of Tennessee, 1891*, 183–184.

15. Clifton, 40.

16. Swint, 10.

17. Ibid.

18. Fletch Coke, "Profiles of John Overton: Judge, Friend, Family Man, and Master of Travellers' Rest." *Tennessee Historical Quarterly* 37, no. 4 (1978): 393–409, http://jstor.org/stable/42625908.

19. Swint, 10.

20. Coke, 401.

21. P'Pool, 9.

22. Ibid, 13.

23. Swint, 11.

24. Ibid., 12.

25. General Edmund W. Pettus went on to become U.S. Senator from Alabama, and the Grand Dragon of the Alabama Ku Klux Klan. The Edmund Pettus bridge in Selma, AL, of civil rights fame, was named for him. See https://www.smithsonianmag.com/history/who-was-edmund-pettus-180954501/, accessed January 21, 2022.

26. I am indebted to Jim Kay, Executive Director, Battle of Nashville Trust, for his insights as we walked the church property on August 11, 2021.

27. John Bell Hood, *Advance and Retreat* (New Orleans, 1880), 303.

28. Mark Zimmerman, *Guide to Civil War Nashville* (Nashville, TN: Battle of Nashville Preservation Society, 2004), 58.

29 ROD, Book 110, 607–608.

30. See https://www.historictravellersrest.org, accessed January 20, 2022.

31. ROD, Book 2, 171, and Book 7, 366–367. These documents describe the "Overton Park Subdivision" on the south side of Tyne Blvd. at Franklin Road, the lands which eventually gave rise to the Holy Trinity Greek Orthodox Church property, the Treemont Development, and to many homes. All of the First Presbyterian Church neighborhood had similar covenants.

Chapter Three
Van Leer Kirkman's Purchase & Era

1. Davidson County Register of Deeds, Book 110, 607–8.

2. ROD, Book 102, 454–5. This is the same tract as that found in Book 27, 260–1 and Book 42, 243.

3. Kenneth P'Pool, John Overton: Appendix with title "Travelers Rest," unnumbered page in *Land owner and developer*, unpublished paper, 1978.

4. Octavia Zollicoffer Bond, "Yester Nashville Names: The Kirkman Family," *Nashville American*, August 29, 1909.

5. "Daring Beauties and the Houses They Built", *Tennessean*, May 9, 1976, Section F.

6. Ibid.

7. "The Late Mrs. Samuella D. Kirkman", *Nashville Daily American*, November 25, 1880.

8. *Tennessean*, "Daring Beauties."

9. The whole story of Jacob Thompson's life and career is quite an adventure. It is well-told in *Accused: A Biography of Jacob Thompson*, Steve Cockerham (Oxford, MS, Triton Press, 2018).

10. The Glen Leven house and the remaining 65 acres of the former estate was given to The Land Trust for Tennessee in 2006. The story of Glen Leven can be found in *Glen Leven Farm: A Family Story*, Ophelia Thompson Paine, (Tree of Life Memoirs: Sewanee, TN, 2016).

11. "Leading Citizens Series: Mr. V. L. Kirkman," *The Chat* (Nashville) 1895, 10.

12. *Munsey's Magazine*, xvi, October 1896–March 1897, (Frank Munsey: New York, 1897): 696.

13. "Nashvillians who will take the train to Memphis for Van Leer Kirkman Wedding," *Nashville Daily American*, December 27, 1886.

14. Ann Toplovich, "Kate Thompson & Van Leer Kirkman: A Brilliant and Noted Wedding, December 30, 1886," blog post at https://tennesseehistory.org/kate-thompson-van-leer-kirkman-brilliant-noted-wedding-december-30-1886/; December 29, 2017, accessed April 29, 2021.

15. Ibid.

16. Mary Hamilton Thompson Orr (1879–1968), unpublished interviews; interviewed by Joe Thompson Jr. in 1958, 1963.

17. This idea came from former historian at Travellers Rest, Lauren Batte, in a conversation with the author at her TR office, 2018.

18. The whole Hermitage Stud story is told in Margaret Lindsley Warden's, "Long-Departed Glory," *Tennessean* magazine, September 12, 1948.

19. James E. Caldwell, *Recollections of a Lifetime*, (Baird–Ward Press: Nashville, TN), 1923.

20. W. Clark Conn, "Waverly Place: The Study of a Nashville Streetcar Suburb Along the Franklin Pike," *Tennessee Historical Quarterly*, 43, no. 1. (1984): 8.

21. *Nashville Daily American*, October 9, 1887, 14. Quote is by Hamilton Busbey.

22. *Nashville in the 1890s*, ed. William Waller (Vanderbilt University Press: Nashville, 1970), 107.

23. Ibid.

24. *Nashville American*, June 24, 1897.

25. Jefferson Davis, *The Papers of Jefferson Davis: 14, 1880–1889*, ed. Lynda Lasswell Crist (Louisiana State University Press: Baton Rouge, 2015), footnote #6.

26. *Nashville in the 1890s*, 106.

27. Ibid., 106–115.

28. Ibid.

29. This subject is pursued in *Woman's Place on Exhibit: Women at the Tennessee Centennial Exposition 1897*; Holly Rogers, Master's thesis, Middle Tennessee State University Dept. of History, Middle Tennessee State University, 2018.

30. "Corner of Rose Garden at Oak Hill", *Nashville American*, May 15, 1919, A-8.

31. "Twelve Trips Made Each Way: Interurban Does Big Business on First Day," *Nashville American*, May 2, 1909.

32. *Nashville Tennessean*, January 29, 1911.

33. *Nashville Tennessean*, January 30, 1911.

34. "Edwin Warner Home Sold for $55,000: Mrs. Van Leer Kirkman is Buyer After Selling Famous Oak Hill," *Tennessean*, January 21, 1923.

35. Ridley Wills II, *Nashville Pikes 3: 150 Years Along Harding Pike* (Ridley Wills II: Nashville, 2017), 97–99.

36. "Mrs. Kate Thompson Kirkman, Civic, and Social Leader; Descendant of Distinguished Family, Dies Here," *Tennessean*, March 24, 1926.

37. The author has visited the Van Leer site, which has quite a few people interred. Nearby is Van Leer Kirkman's sister, Mary Frances Kirkman Drouillard, the Nashville socialite who married the Union soldier and caused such a stir.

Chapter Four
The Rogers Caldwell Years

1. *Tennessean*, May 25, 1924.

2. *Davidson County Register of Deeds*, Book 700, 39–44.

3. "A Rich Man's Son Earns His Own Success," article in *The New South*, March 1927, 23.

4. Idem.

5. "Rogers Caldwell Dies After Brief Illness," *Nashville Banner*, October 9, 1968.

6. "The Rogers Caldwell Story," George Barker, *Nashville Tennessean Magazine*, 1963.

7. "The Rise and Fall of the House of Caldwell," Don H. Doyle, subchapter of chapter "On the Wall Street of the South," *Nashville in the New South 1880–1930* (1985, University of Tennessee), p 223–232.

8. Ibid., quoting *Tennessean*, July 18, 1928.

9. Ibid.

10. When the author, in 2018 interview, asked Caldwell descendant Meredith Caldwell, III, why he thought Rogers Caldwell would buy such a lavish estate as the Kirkman Oak Hill Farm, just to have a place to live for a short while, he answered, "Probably because he could!"

11. Shirley Caldwell-Patterson, *The Patriarch, Caldwell & Company, and Me, Shirley* (Nashville: Churchill/Black, 2021) 158.

12. *Tennessean*, May 9, 1926.

13. *Tennessean*, October 26, 1926.

14. "History of the Ellington Center," Tennessee Department of Agriculture web site.

15. Jesse Hill Ford, *Mr. Potter and His Bank* (Nashville: Commerce Union Bank, 1977), 34–46.

16. Doyle, *Nashville in the New South*, 231.
17. ROD, Book 737, 81–83.

Chapter Five
The Cheek Family Years

1. *The International Confectioner*, January, 1923, 18.
2. W. A. Gibson Jr., "Poster Advertising Plays Important Part in Sales Building for Maxwell House Coffee," *The Poster*, 13, no. 1 (January, 1922), 23.
3. "Joel Owsley Cheek", in *Encyclopedia of Biography*, article in "Cheek" folder, vertical files of Tennessee State Library and Archives.
4. "Good Since the First Drop," *Tennessean*, January 4, 1976.
5. "Don't Quote Me" society column, *Tennessean*, July 30, 1930.
6. Quitclaim info from First Presbyterian Church archives.
7. Matt DeLorenz, *Dodge 100 Years*, (Minneapolis: Motorbooks, 2014).
8. *Nashville Pikes 3: 150 Years Along Harding Pike*, Ridley Wills II, 192.
9. "Peabody Aid Society Meets Friday With Mrs. John Cheek as Hostess," *Tennessean*, October 27, 1934. This article speaks of "the new home" of the Cheeks.
10. First Presbyterian Church of Nashville, Sunday worship bulletin, April 24, 1949.
11. "John Cheek Home May Become Our Youth Center," *The Old First Forum* 2, no. 6 (May 1949), First Presbyterian Church, Nashville, Tenn. Also see "Oak Hill Chapel and Church House," booklet published by the church after the Cheek purchase.

Chapter Six
First Presbyterian Church of Nashville

1. 'My Years as Minister of First Presbyterian Church, Nashville, Tennessee." Walter Rowe Courtenay, 1984 (1985?), recollection. First Presbyterian Church Archives.
2. This remarkably thorough booklet bears the full title of *Reports of the Building Survey Committee as Presented to the Congregational Meeting, First Presbyterian Church, Nashville, Tennessee*, October 24, 1944.
3. Steele, *First Church* 2, 166.
4. Courtenay, "My Years …"
5. "Church to Buy Oak Hill Estate, *Tennessean*, May 2, 1949.

6. Letter from Allen Dobson to Alf Adams, Henry Boyd, Wilbur Creighton, Jr., Sam L. Fleming, Dr. Oren A. Oliver, and R. D. Stanford Jr., May 9, 1949. From church archives.

7. Untitled 1949 brochure. From church archives.

8. Steele 2, 175–179.

9. Ibid., 179.

10. First Presbyterian Church Session Minutes, October 1954.

11. Steele 2, 181.

12. First Presbyterian Church Session Minutes, October 1954.

13. Steele 2, 187.

Chapter Seven
Take a Look Around

1. I am grateful to Hill McAlister for personal discussions about the flagpole and about his family's long-term Nashville connections.

2. Ridley Wills II, *Nashville Pikes 1: 150 Years Along Franklin Pike and Granny White Pike* (Ridley Wills II, Nashville, TN, 2015), 217.

3. Most of this information comes from "Turnpikes and Bridges in Davidson County, TN," in Nashvillehistory.blogspot.com, published July 6, 2014, accessed by author last on November 11, 2021. The blog itself quotes extensively from *History of Nashville, Tennessee*, H. W. Crew, (Publishing House of the Methodist Episcopal Church, South, Barbee and Smith, Agents, Nashville, TN, 1890).

4. Ridley Wills, II, Preface to *Nashville Pikes*, xvi.

5. Davidson County Register of Deeds, Book 2693, 475, Negley family to Davidson Co. Board of Education; see also Cheek to Negley, Bk 1163, 544.

6. ROD, Book 3794, 575–578.

7. Ridley Wills, II, *Pikes* 1, 6–7.

8. ROD, Plan Book 2, 171.

9. The 1936 deed is in Book 1021, 9; 1949 deed, Book 1715, 513; 1961 deed, Book 327, 342; and 1977 deed, Book 5104, 785.

10. "A Brief History of the Holy Trinity Greek Orthodox Church," www.holytrinitynashville.org, accessed 11/21/21.

11. Personal interview with Patricia Potter McDonald, 2019. The Beauvoir home had five bedrooms and five bathrooms. It burned in the 1970s. Mrs. McDonald sold other parts of the Beauvoir property to the Treemont Development Co. in the

1980s as Co-Trustee (with her sister Jean Potter McCann) for their deceased father, Edward Potter Jr.

12. ROD, Plan, Book 2, 171.

13. Ridley Wills II, *Nashville Streets and Their Stories* (Plumbline Media: Franklin, TN, 2012) 150.

14. ROD, Courtenay to Gladys P. Stahlman, Book 2540, 385; Book 2799, 502–504.

15. Much more about Edward Potter, Jr. and that family can be found in *Mr. Potter and His Bank*, Jesse Hill Ford (Nashville: Commerce Union Bank, 1977).

16. ROD, Book 6250, 896.

17. Hugh Walker, "Kirkman Lane: Link With Carriage Days", *Tennessean*, July 1, 1979, and *Tennessean*, "Approval Remains on Kirkman Lane," July 12, 1979.

18. Quit Claim Deed of Consolidation, Instrument #20210921–0126955, September 21, 2021.

19. ROD, Plat Book 1835, 15–16.

20. "E. L. McNeilly Robertson Academy Legal Correspondence," folder in Special Collections Division, Main Library, Metro Nashville Public Library. Documents and summaries in this file represent extensive legal research by attorney E. L. McNeilly in 1911, and forwarded by McNeilly and Henry E. Colton to Joseph Thompson in 1930. Thompson was President of the Trustees of Robertson Academy. Some correspondence seems to be about whether the Trustees can sell or dispose of the land and under what circumstances.

21. Ridley Wills, II, *Pikes*, 1, citing a Mary Maxwell (Mollie) Claiborne unpublished manuscript, "Maxwell Hall, account of Maxwell family in Tennessee," J. M. Dickinson Papers, manuscript section, Archives Division, Tennessee State Library and Archives.

22. "E. L. McNeilly Robertson Academy Legal Correspondence," folder in Special Collections Division, Main Library, Metro Nashville Public Library.

23. ROD, Plan Book 5, 8.

24. "Robertson Academy, First School of County, Has Interesting History," *Tennessean*, March 20, 1922.

25. "Robertson Chapter Will Present Portrait of Nashville's Founder to Robertson Academy," *Tennessean*, April 19, 1925. The "Caldwell estate" mentioned would be that of Rogers Caldwell, whose Brentwood Hall was being built at the time of this article.

26. Margaret Lindsley Warden, "Dobbin's Due," *Tennessean Magazine*, May 13, 1956.

27. "Report of Robertson Academy Trustees to Tennessee General Assembly," October 29, 1827. Record Group 60, Box 101, Folder 7. Courtesy of Tennessee State Library and Archives.

28. John L. Craig, "Life at Old Robertson Academy," *Nashville Banner*, June 2, 1935.

29. Minutes of Chancery Court, Davidson County, Book 78, 400ff and 500ff.

30. Ibid.

31. Ibid.

32. ROD, Book 1229, 60–62.

33. Interview by author of Lavinia Jones Fillebrown, May 2017. She is granddaughter of Robert Franklin Jones, daughter of Ralph Culbert Jones. She lived for several years in the house her grandfather built. At this writing, she lives at The Blakeford in Nashville. Her daughter and son-in-law, Tim Vaughn, are First Presbyterian members.

34. I was fortunate that a history of Franklin Road Academy had just been written when the present book was being written. It is *The Start of Franklin Road Academy: Context and History*, Clinton J. Holloway (Nashville, TN, 2020), privately printed. Personal discussions with Dr. Holloway have enriched the research, as well.

Bibliography

Acklen, Jeanette Tillotson, et al. eds. Bible Records and Marriage Bonds. Heritage Books, 2007.

Arnow, Harriette Simpson. *Flowering of the Cumberland*. New York: Macmillan Company, 1963.

———. *Seedtime on the Cumberland*. Lincoln: University of Nebraska Press, 1960.

Bucy, Carole. *Nashville 101*. Public lecture by Davidson County's Historian.

Caldwell, James E. *Recollections of a Lifetime*. Nashville: Baird-Ward Press, 1923.

Caldwell, Mary French. *Tennessee, the Dangerous Example, Watauga to 1849*. Knoxville, TN: Aurora Publications, 1974.

Caldwell-Patterson, Shirley. *The Patriarch, Caldwell and Company, and Me, Shirley*. Nashville, TN: Churchill/Black, 2021.

The Chat. Periodical. Nashville: 1895.

Claiborne, Mary Maxwell (Mollie). *A History of the Jesse Maxwell Family in Tennessee*. Nashville: unpublished manuscript, 1929.

Clements, Paul. *Chronicles of the Cumberland Settlements 1779–1796*. Nashville, TN: The Foundation of William and Jennifer Frist, and Paul Clements, self-published, 2012.

Clifton, Frances. "John Overton as Andrew Jackson's Friend." *Tennessee Historical Quarterly* II, no. 1 (March 1952).

Cockerham, Steve. *A Biography of Jacob Thompson*. Oxford, MS: Triton Press, 2018.

Courtenay, Walter Rowe. "My Years As Minister of First Presbyterian Church, Nashville, Tennessee." Memoir in First Presbyterian Church Archives, 1984 or 1985.

Coke, Fletch. "Profiles of John Overton: Judge, Friend, Family Man, and Master of Travellers Rest. *Tennessee Historical Quarterly*, 37, no. 4 (1978).

Conn, W. Clark. "Waverly Place: The Study of a Nashville Streetcar Suburb Along the Franklin Pike." *Tennessee Historical Quarterly*, 43, no. 1 (1984).

Confederate Veteran. 3, no. 6, June 1895.

Creighton, Wilbur, Jr. and Leland R. Johnson. *The First Presbyterian Church of Nashville: A Documentary History.* Nashville: First Presbyterian Church,1986.

Crew, H. W. *History of Nashville, Tennessee.* Nashville: Publishing House of the Methodist Episcopal Church, South, 1890.

Davidson County Register of Deeds Office.

Davis, Jefferson. *The Papers of Jefferson Davis: 14, 1880–1889,* ed. Linda Lasswell Crist. Baton Rouge, LA: Louisiana State University Press, 2015.

DeLorenz, Matt. *Dodge 100 Years.* 2014.

Dixon, Max. *The Wataugans.* Johnson City, TN: The Overmountain Press, 1989.

Doyle, Don H. Nashville in the New South 1880-1930. Knoxville, TN: University of Tennessee Press, 1985.

Drake, Doug, Jack Masters and Bill Puryear. *Founding of the Cumberland Settlements: The First Atlas, 1779–1804.* Gallatin,TN: Warioto Press, 2009.

Dykeman, Wilma. *Tennessee, A Bicentennial History.* Nashville: American Association for State and Local History, 1975.

Ford, Jesse Hill. *Mister Potter and His Bank: A Life of Edward Potter, Jr.* Nashville: Commerce Union Bank, 1977.

Griffey, Irene M. *The Preemptors—Middle Tennessee's First Settlers—volume 1 of a Series of Early Tennessee Land Records.* Clarksville, TN: Irene M. Griffey, 1989.

History of Homes and Gardens of Tennessee. Compiled by The Garden Study Club of Nashville: ed. Roberta Seawell Brandau. Nashville: Parthenon Press, 1936; renewed 1964; reprinted by Friends of Cheekwood, 1974.

Holloway, Clinton J. *The Start of Franklin Road Academy: Context and History.* Privately printed. Nashville: 2020.

Hood, John Bell. *Advance and Retreat.* New Orleans, 1880.

The International Confectioner. January 1923.

McFerrin, John Berry. *Caldwell and Company: A Southern Financial Empire.* Raleigh: University of North Carolina Press, 1939; reissued Vanderbilt University Press, 1969.

Masters, Jack and Bill Puryear. *Thoroughfare for Freedom: The Second Atlas of the Cumberland Settlements, 1779–1804.* Gallatin, TN: Warioto Press, 2011.

———. *The First Southwest: The Third Atlas of the Cumberland and Duck River Settlements.* Gallatin, TN: Warioto Press, 2012.

Munsey's Magazine xvi, October 1896–March 1897. New York: Frank Munsey, 1897.

Nashville Banner.

Nashville Daily American.

Nashville Tennessean.

Nashville Public Library. *Nashville: A Family Town*, 1978.

The New South. "A Rich Man Earns His Own Success." March 1927.

The Poster 13, no. 1, January 1922.

Paine, Ophelia Thompson. *Glen Leven Farm: A Family Story.* Sewanee, TN: Patricia West/Tree of Life Memoirs, 2016.

P'Pool, Kenneth. John Overton: *Landowner and Developer.* Nashville: unpublished paper, 1978; courtesy Historic Travellers Rest.

Ray, Kristofer. *Middle Tennessee 1775–1825: Progress and Popular Democracy on the Southwestern Frontier.* Knoxville: University of Tennessee Press, 2007.

Rogers, Holly. *Woman's Place on Exhibit: Women in the Tennessee Centennial Exposition 1897.* Master's thesis, Middle Tennessee State University, 2018.

Steele, Damaris Witherspoon. *First Church: A History of Nashville First Presbyterian Church*, 1, 2, 3. Nashville: First Presbyterian Church, 2004, 2005.

Swint, Henry Lee. "Travellers Rest: Home of Judge John Overton." Nashville: *Tennessee Historical Quarterly* xxvi (Spring 1967).

Tennessee Department of Agriculture web site. "History of the Ellington Center."

Tennessee Encyclopedia of History and Culture. Nashville: Rutledge Hill Press with Tennessee Historical Society, 1998.

Tennessee Historical Quarterly 26, Spring, 1967. Nashville: Tennessee Historical Commission.

West, Nan Overton, compiler. *The Overtons: 700 Years.* 1998.

Waller, William, ed. *Nashville in the 1890s.* Nashville: Vanderbilt University Press, 1970.

———. *Nashville: 1900-1910.* Nashville: Vanderbilt University Press, 1972.

Wills, Jesse. *Reports of the Building Survey Committee as Presented to the Congregational Meeting, First Presbyterian Church, Nashville, Tennessee, October 24, 1944.*

Wills, Ridley II. *Nashville Pikes, 1, 150 Years Along Franklin Pike and Granny White Pike.* Nashville, TN: Ridley Wills II, 2015.

———. *Nashville Pikes 2, 150 Years Along the Hillsboro Pike*. Nashville: Ridley Wills II.

———. *Nashville Pikes 3, 150 Years Along Harding Pike*. Nashville: Ridley Wills II, 2017.

———. *Nashville Streets and Their Stories*. Franklin, TN: Plumbline Media, 2012.

Yalobusha County Historical Society Minutes [Yalobusha County, MS]. Minutes of October 12, 2012.

Zimmerman, Mark. *Guide to Civil War Nashville*. Nashville: Battle of Nashville Preservation Society, 2004.

Index

B

Barr, Thomas Calhoun 72, 73
   First Presbyterian Church divides, 1942 74
Battle of Franklin 22, 23
Battle of King's Mountain 6, 10
Battle of Nashville 18, 22, 23, 45, 97, 102, 113
   First Presbyterian Church used as a Federal hospital 24
Battle of Peach Orchard Hill 25
Bean, William 6
Beauvoir 99–101
Belle Vue 40
Berry, William T. 32, 40
Bledsoe, Anthony 6, 9
Boone, Daniel 6, 7
Braeburn 63
Brentwood Academy 113
Bridle Path, the 102
Bryant, William T. 118
Building Survey Committee, 1940s,
   First Presbyterian Church 75, 76
      congregational survey, January 1948 77

Conover, Dr., consultant to Building Survey Committee 75, 76
   report from Hart, Freeland, and Roberts architects, 1949 79

C

Caldwell, James E. 40, 53, 55, 57, 96, 106
Caldwell, Margaret Trousdale (wife of Rogers Caldwell) 57
Caldwell, May Winston (wife of James E. Caldwell) 53
Caldwell, Rogers 51, 53, 56, 57, 59, 60, 96, 106
   Bank of Tennessee 56, 57
   Brentwood Hall 57, 58, 96, 106
   Caldwell and Company 56–58, 61
   empire tumbled in 1929 57
   newspaper quote, 1928 56
Cheek, Elizabeth Hale (first wife of Frank L. Cheek) 59
Cheek, Frank L. 58–61
Cheek House 25, 38, 61, 63, 82, 84, 85, 89
Cheek, Joel Owsley 58, 59, 62
Cheek, John Hancock 61, 62, 71

138 INDEX

Cheek, Marie Walters (second wife of Frank L. Cheek) 59, 61
Cheek-Neal Coffee Company 58, 60, 62, 95
Cheek, Susan Glenn 72, 103
Chickamauga 7
church flagpole inscription; McAllister family 95
Claiborne, Mollie Maxwell 11
Claiborne memoir 10, 13, 106
Claiborne, Mrs. Thomas (née Ann Maxwell) 107
Col. John Overton 21, 26, 29, 38, 39, 46, 61, 98, 99, 102, 110, 113
committee to renovate and expand, 1948 77
Cooper, Cortez 118
County Donegal, Ireland 11
Courtenay, Walter Rowe 55, 74, 75, 100, 117
"The Future of Old First," sermon 76
Crieve Hall 60, 99
Cumberland Compact 6, 10
Cumberland Motor Company, Inc. 62
Cumberland settlements 1, 7, 11, 14

D
Demonbreun, Timothy 7
Dickinson, Jacob McGavock (great-grandson of Judge John Overton) 26
Dickinson, Martha M. Overton (daughter of Col. John Overton) 98
Donelson flotilla 8

Donelson, John 7, 9, 13, 18
dry-stacked walls; historical marker #132 97

E
Eason, Susan Anderson Cheek (wife to William H. Eason) 103
Eason, William Howard 72, 103
property purchased in 2010 by First Presbyterian Church 72
Ellington Agricultural Center 58, 96, 106, 107

F
Father of Middle Tennessee 6. *See also* Robertson, James
Floral Parade, the 45. *See also* Kirkman, Katherine (Kate) Thompson (Van Leer Kirkman's second wife)
Franklin Road Academy (FRA) 113
Franklin Turnpike 18, 29, 38, 96, 97, 111
Franklin Turnpike Company 18, 96
French and Indian War 2, 3, 14

G
Glendale Park 40, 53, 54, 106
Glen Leven 18, 34, 38, 53, 82, 98, 110, 116
Golgotha (first name for Travellers Rest) 16

H
Harding, Rachel (wife of Judge John Overton) 21
Harding, Thomas 21
Hartsfield, William 105–107

Henderson, Richard 6, 7
Hermitage Stud 39, 110
Holy Trinity Greek Orthodox Church 98–101
Hood, General John Bell 23, 25

J
Jackson, Andrew 13, 14, 18, 20, 31, 58
Jackson-Overton friendship 13, 18–20
John Overton High School 98, 113
John Overton Jr. 18, 22
Jones, Todd B. 119
Judson Baptist Church 98

K
Kirkman, Eleanora Chambers Van Leer (mother to Van Leer Kirkman) 31
Kirkman, Ella and Hugh (children of Van Leer Kirkman and first wife, Samuella) 32
Kirkman house 31
Kirkman, Hugh (father to Van Leer Kirkman) 31, 33
Kirkman, Katherine (Kate) Thompson (Van Leer Kirkman's second wife) 33
    1897 description from a national magazine 34
    Kate Kirkman Day 45
Kirkman Lane 101, 102, 103
Kirkman, Mary Florence (sibling to Van Leer Kirkman) 31, 32, 35

Kirkman, Samuella Berry (Van Leer Kirkman's first wife) 32, 33, 35, 40, 49
    obituary 32
Kirkman, Van Leer 26, 29, 31, 34–40, 46, 48, 49, 51, 54, 56, 97, 102, 110, 111, 115
    December 30, 1886, description of wedding 35
    description of Kirkman from a Nashville periodical 34

L
Land Grants 8, 61
    Land Grant #60 16, 29, 38
    Land Grant #367 12, 13, 16, 22, 26, 29, 61, 96
    Land Grant #390 29
    Lytle land grant 31
    Rice, John, 1783 land grant 20
Lea Elizabeth B. Overton (daughter to Judge John Overton) 101
Lea, Judge John M. 101, 102
Lealand Lane. *See also* Lea, Judge John M.
Lee, General Stephen D. 25
Longview, the Caldwell estate 54

M
Major Buildings and Projects: 1934–2022 88
Maxwell, David 8, 9, 10, 11, 12, 61, 96, 116
Maxwell House Coffee 59–61, 63
Maxwell House Hotel 46, 60, 61
Maxwell, Jesse 8–10

Maxwell, Martha A. Claiborne (wife of Jessee Maxwell Jr.) 61
Maxwell, William and Moses 12, 13, 29, 85
Memphis, creation by Judge John Overton 20
military district 9
Moore, Ryan V. 120

N
Narthex plaques honoring James I. Vance, John Todd Edgar, and Thomas V. Moore 84
Nashville Centennial, April 24, 1880 8
Nashville Coffee and Manufacturing Company 59
Nashville Junto, the 19
Nashville Thompsons 34
Native American Indians 1, 2, 3
   Cherokee 6, 7
   Chickasaw tribe 20
   Chief Attakullakulla 7
   Dragging Canoe 7

O
Oak Hill (Cheek) 63
Oak Hill (Harding family estate) 22
Oak Hill (Kirkman) 34, 39
   Field and Farm magazine description 43
Oak Hill Subdivision 53
Oak Hill (the city) 27
Oak Hill Valley Subdivision 103, 105
old stone wall historical marker; 1864 Battle of Nashville story 102

Orr, Mary Hamilton Thompson, interview 38
Overmountain Colony 6. *See also* Watauga Association
Overmountain Men 6
Overton, Col. John. *See also* Overton, John Jr.
Overton Hall 60, 99
Overton, Harriet Virginia Maxwell (wife of Col. John Overton) 22, 26, 29, 38, 61
Overton, John Jr. 18, 22
   leadership duties at Travellers Rest 22
Overton, Judge John 12, 13, 18, 20, 29, 38, 61, 85, 96, 101, 113, 116
Overton, Mary McConnell (White) May, wife of Judge John Overton 17, 21, 110
Overton, May (son of Col. John and Harriet Overton) 26, 35, 39, 113
Overton Park 98, 100
Overton, Robert L. 39
Overton, Sarah "Saidee" Williams. *See also* Overton Hall

P
Potter, Catherine Jane Tyne 100
Potter, Edward Jr. 100, 101
Preemptions 8
Proclamation of 1763 3, 6
Purchase of Cheek property, 1949 71, 78
   booklet describing property and church's plans for the future 79

events that led to the purchase 72
newspaper coverage of the May 1 congregational vote 78

R

Relocation 81
   a congregation divided 81
   bids for the sale of the downtown property 83
   complaint to the Nashville Presbytery 82
   long-range planning survey 80
   Moving Pains 83
   resolution to relocate 82
   sale of the downtown property 84
   Sunday, June 5, 1955, first worship service and groundbreaking ceremony 84, 85
Robards, Rachel Donelson (Mrs. Andrew Jackson) 14, 19
Robertson Academy 29, 40, 48, 81, 90, 101, 105–107, 110, 111
Robertson, James 6, 7, 9, 16

S

Seven Years' War 2. *See also* French and Indian War
Sevier, John 6
Shelby, Isaac 9
slave-built stone wall built in the 1840s; boundary between Overton and Leas 102
slaveholder, Judge John Overton 17
Snowden, Annie Overton Brinkley (granddaughter of Judge John Overton and Mary White Overton) 31, 38

Snowden purchase 31, 38
Soper, Adele Smith (wife of W. H. Soper) 51
Soper, W. H. 49, 51, 59
   deed for the Soper-to-Caldwell transaction (shows several notable neighbors) 53
Stanford Chapel 80, 89
Sumner property's connection to Col. John Overton 110

T

Tatum, Absolom 9
Tennessee Centennial Exposition of 1897, Kirkman involvement 43
The Ohio Company 1, 2
Thomas J. Tyne 48, 100, 101
Thompson, Caswell Macon 33
Thompson House 33
Thompson, John 35, 39, 105, 110, 111, 115, 116
Thompson, Mary McConnell Overton (Mrs. John Thompson) 39
Transylvania 7
Transylvania Company 7
Travellers Rest 16, 18–22, 24–26, 29, 39, 53, 61, 96–103, 107, 110, 113, 116
   1964 restoration 26
   agricultural operation 17
   Arabian horse farm 26
   covenants 26, 62
   planning headquarters for Jackson's 1824 campaign for the U.S. Presidency 19

use of the estate as Confederate Headquarters 18, 22

Treaty of Paris 3

Treaty of Sycamore Shoals 6, 7

Treemont 100, 101

Tyndall, Thomas 119

Tyne Boulevard 100

Tyne, Thomas J. 100

U

Ulster Plantation experiment 11

V

Vance, Dr. James I. 72

Van Leer, A. W. (Van Leer Kirkman's grandfather) 31

Van Leer obelisk 50

W

Washington, George 2, 48

Watauga 6, 7, 8, 46

Watauga Association 6

Waverly, Nashville suburb 40, 54, 98

Wills, Jesse 75, 76, 77, 83. *See also* Building Survey Committee, 1940s, First Presbyterian Church

The author, Bill Caruso. Courtesy of Bill Caruso.

About the Author

William C. Caruso (Bill) is a Certified Christian Educator in the Presbyterian Church (U.S.A.) denomination. In his career, he served Church Educator positions in churches in Greensboro, NC, Sarasota, Florida, and Nashville, Tennessee. For twenty-two years, Bill was Director of Adult Education at First Presbyterian Church of Nashville. In retirement there, he has been the volunteer historian/archivist for the church. In 2012, the Association of Presbyterian Church Educators gave him the Life Achievement Award.

Bill holds degrees from Emory University, Georgia; Georgia State University, Atlanta; and Union Presbyterian Seminary, Richmond, Virginia. He was the editor of *Appointed to Serve: 100 Years of Memories*, a history of the Assembly's Training School/Presbyterian School of Christian Education. Bill and Bekah Caruso have worked together in various ways in each congregation they served, and both have enjoyed singing in choirs. Bill has been an active Scouting leader for many years. They have a married son and two grandchildren. Bill and Bekah Caruso now live in Black Mountain, North Carolina.

www.ingramcontent.com/pod-product-compliance
Lightning Source LLC
Chambersburg PA
CBHW050727010526
44107CB00009B/765